Math Equals

Biographies
of Women Mathematicians

+ Related Activities

Teri Perl

Addison-Wesley Publishing Company
Menlo Park, California • Reading, Massachusetts
London • Amsterdam • Don Mills, Ontario • Sydney

Acknowledgements

I am very grateful to my friends Karel DeLeeuw and Paul Shields for reading the manuscript and helping check that the mathematics is clear and correct, and to Lenore Blum for sharing the history of American Women in Mathematics and generally encouraging the idea of the book. Flora Russ gave up a beautiful Sunday to look over the material with me and sent me the last hidden mathematicians puzzle, generated by a computer program of her student Michael Mozer. Also special thanks to all of the young people who tried out the material, in particular Louise Dunaway's group at Los Altos High School, to Catherine Franke during a summer at Stanford University, and to my daughter Anne.

This book is in the ADDISON-WESLEY INNOVATIVE SERIES.

ISBN 0-201-05709-3
12 13 14 15 16 17 18 19 20 HA 95949392

Preface

People today are reexamining the roles of women in contemporary society. Science and mathematics, long considered the domain of men, has seemed territory particularly hostile to women. This book has been written to help change that image. It does so by exploring the lives of a number of women who have made significant contributions to mathematics, and by providing an experience of doing mathematics in the context of the work in which they were involved.

The lives of the women included here raise questions about roles of women, and obstacles placed by family and society on the development of the talents of women in general. By dealing with these issues it is hoped that people, both men and women, will become more aware of the forces which have influenced their attitudes in the past. Thus awareness may lead to career choices based more on individual talents and interests, and less on constraints dictated by sex role stereotypes.

A word about the mathematical activities included in the book: they have been chosen as relating to the areas of mathematics in which the women worked. Because many of them deal with topics not usually introduced in early mathematics courses, they may seem difficult. A better way to describe them would be "unfamiliar." Readers of varied mathematical backgrounds should find the activities accessible, since they are not skill based. They are also not sequential in concept or level of difficulty, and so they may be explored out of sequence. I hope the reader will find them interesting, unusual, and in some ways suggestive of the kinds of explorations that make mathematics so fascinating to the mathematician.

Contents

Protesting the granting of degrees to women around 1890, Cambridge undergraduates lower a female effigy on a bicycle out of a bookseller's window.

Access to all university education has been closed to women until surprisingly recently. This has been only one of many obstacles to women making fundamental contributions in areas like mathematics.

Meet the Women

Suppose someone asked you to associate a list of professions or jobs with the word *man* or *woman*. The result would probably look like this: doctor—man; gardener—man; nurse—woman; elementary school teacher—woman; college teacher—man; astronaut—man; telephone operator—woman; electrician—man; mathematician—_____ .
Surely most people would put *man* next to *mathematician*. It is one of many occupations that very few women have entered. Why this is so is not yet clear. Most evidence points to a complex set of reasons, mainly rooted in roles which society assigns both men and women.

Mathematicians in general are a little known group; women mathematicians even less known. Table 1-1 shows a list of names of both men and women mathematicians concealed in the Hidden Mathematicians puzzle on page 2. The names of the nine women discussed in this book are hidden with the others. In column A beside the list, write *W* if you think the name belonged to a woman, *M* if you think it was a man. This may be easier than you think. If you recognize the name at all, you're probably correct in guessing that it belonged to a man. Some of the ones you've never heard of belonged to women. Try it, and see how many times you are correct.

Notice also that the rows and columns in the puzzle have been numbered; there are sixteen of each. This makes it easy to communicate the location of names. Write the row and column in which the name starts in column B, and the row and column in which it ends in column C. For example, *Fourier* appears horizontally starting in the thirteenth row of the tenth column. Thus the entry in column B is (13,10). The last letter is located at (13,16), as shown in column C. Now do the puzzle, completing columns B and C as you go.

Hidden Mathematicians Puzzle

Column
↓

Row →	1	2	3	4	5	6	7	8	9	10	11	12	13	14	15	16
1	A	K	I	M	O	C	R	A	E	Y	O	U	N	G	A	E
2	L	O	V	E	L	A	C	E	T	R	O	D	O	E	F	U
3	N	V	L	O	M	U	G	R	A	G	E	U	C	L	I	D
4	E	A	A	R	U	C	E	N	D	A	S	C	N	I	B	O
5	R	L	P	R	T	H	S	O	E	M	O	H	A	G	O	X
6	O	E	L	I	H	Y	T	E	S	S	E	A	R	O	N	U
7	A	V	A	E	E	S	I	T	C	R	I	T	G	U	A	S
8	R	S	C	M	O	R	E	H	A	O	N	E	A	G	C	C
9	C	K	E	A	S	O	M	E	R	V	I	L	L	E	C	A
10	H	A	A	N	P	I	E	R	T	H	A	E	O	R	I	N
11	I	Y	P	N	L	A	T	H	E	O	N	T	I	M	A	T
12	M	A	P	L	A	S	S	G	S	Y	E	A	S	A	M	O
13	E	D	L	A	B	E	L	C	A	F.	O	U	R	I	E	R
14	D	N	E	W	T	O	N	O	A	U	V	I	L	N	A	E
15	E	V	A	N	S	I	A	M	E	L	S	O	N	E	O	R
16	S	D	I	O	P	H	A	N	T	U	S	S	E	O	R	E

Table 1-1.

	A (*W,M*)	B (Row, Column)	C (Row, Column)		A (*W,M*)	B (Row, Column)	C (Row, Column)
Abel	_____	_____	_____	Germain	_____	_____	_____
Agnesi	_____	_____	_____	Hypatia	_____	_____	_____
Archimedes	_____	_____	_____	Kovalevskaya	_____	_____	_____
Cantor	_____	_____	_____	Laplace	_____	_____	(9,3)
Cauchy	_____	_____	_____	Lovelace	_____	_____	_____
Descartes	_____	_____	_____	Napier	_____	_____	_____
Diophantus	M	(16,2)	_____	Newton	_____	_____	_____
Du Châtelet	_____	_____	_____	Noether	_____	_____	_____
Euclid	_____	_____	_____	Pascal	_____	_____	_____
Eudoxus	_____	_____	_____	Riemann	_____	_____	_____
Euler	_____	_____	_____	Somerville	_____	_____	_____
Fibonacci	_____	_____	_____	Theon	_____	_____	_____
Fourier	M	(13,10)	(13,16)	Young, G. C.	_____	_____	_____
Galois	_____	_____	_____	Young, W. H.	_____	_____	_____
Gauss	_____	_____	_____				

Let's Get to Know Them

The following activity will help you look more closely at the unfamiliar names of these women mathematicians while at the same time practicing the important mathematical concepts of *prime* and *composite* numbers. A *prime number* is a number which has only itself and 1 as factors. A *composite number* is any number that can be expressed by multiplying together two or more prime numbers. For example, 12 is a composite number because it can be expressed as 3 X 4 or 6 X 2 as well as 12 X 1. 11 is a prime number since it can only be expressed as 11 X 1.

15 is a _____ number because it can be expressed as _____ X _____ as well as _____ X _____ .

Look at the women mathematicians' names shown in Table 1-2. Count the number of letters in each first name. Count the number of letters in each last name. Fill in the figure.

Table 1-2.

	Number of letters in first name	Prime or Com- posite?	Number of letters in last name	Prime or Com- posite?	Number of letters in complete name	Prime or Com- posite?
Hypatia						
Emilie du Châtelet						
Maria Agnesi						
Sophie Germain						
Mary Somerville						
Ada Lovelace						
Sonya Kovalevskaya						
Grace Young						
Emmy Noether						

Let P_1 be the set of women mathematicians' names in which the first name contains a prime number of letters. List the names in set P_1.

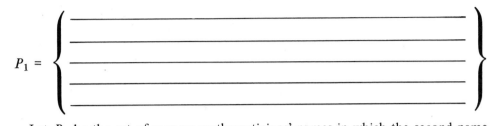

$$P_1 = \left\{ \underline{\hspace{8cm}} \right\}$$

Let P_2 be the set of women mathematicians' names in which the second name contains a prime number of letters. List the names in set P_2.

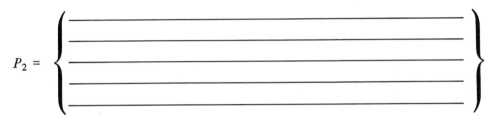

$$P_2 = \left\{ \underline{\hspace{8cm}} \right\}$$

Using sets P_1 and P_2, fill in the Venn diagram* (Figure 1-1).

In region A, write the names of the women mathematicians whose first names contain a prime number of letters; that is, the members of the set P_1.

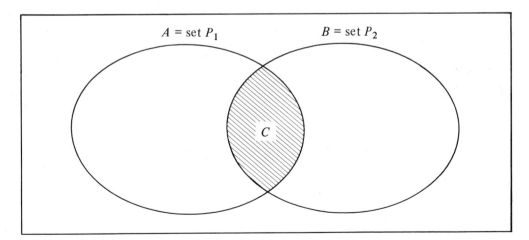

A = set P_1 B = set P_2

C

Figure 1-1.

---

*For additional information on Venn Diagrams, see Appendix 1.

In region B, write the names of the women mathematicians whose last names contain a prime number of letters; that is, the members of the set P_2.

What do you guess should happen in region C? Note that it will not be empty in this example. All the names in region C have prime numbers of letters in both first *and* second names.

How many names are in region A? _____

How many names are in region B? _____

How many names are in region C? _____

Region C is called the intersection of sets P_1 and P_2. In set language it is written with a special symbol $\cap$. We write $C = A \cap B$.

Figure 1-2 below is a Venn Diagram that classifies the information in Table 1-2 into **three** sets and their various intersections. Sets P_1 and P_2 are defined as before. Set P_3 is new. This is the set of women mathematicians' names in which the complete name contains a prime number of letters. List the names in set P_3.

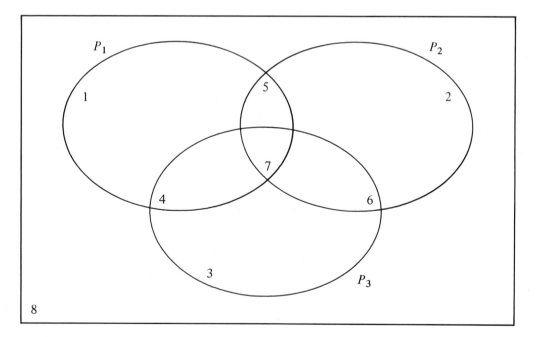

Figure 1-2.

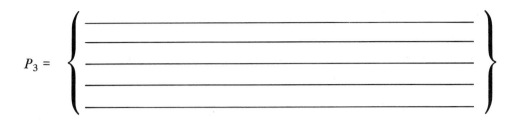

$$P_3 = \left\{ \begin{array}{c} \rule{7cm}{0.4pt} \\ \rule{7cm}{0.4pt} \\ \rule{7cm}{0.4pt} \\ \rule{7cm}{0.4pt} \\ \rule{7cm}{0.4pt} \end{array} \right\}$$

Notice that the diagram is much more complex now.

The Venn diagram in Figure 1-1 contained _____ regions. This three-set Venn diagram divides the space into _____ regions.

See if you can place the names of the women mathematicians in the three-set Venn diagram in Figure 1-2.

Notice that four regions are empty. In particular, region 7 is empty. Region 7 is the intersection of P_1, P_2, and P_3. It will almost always be empty for this kind of classification. Why?

Hypatia

Books on the history of mathematics contain few women's names. Hypatia is usually the first of these. Hypatia lived and worked in Alexandria, in an era when that city was a great center of Greek intellectual life. The city had been built by Alexander the Great, conqueror of Greece, Asia Minor, and Egypt. It had been built in a lovely setting on the Mediterranean Sea, near one mouth of the River Nile. Alexander had planned it to be the most magnificent city in the world, and many who saw it reported that it was. After Alexander's death in 323 B.C., his empire was divided. Ptolemy became the ruler of Egypt: he chose Alexandria to be the capital of his kingdom.

In Alexandria Ptolemy founded a university. This was the first university in the sense that we use the word today. To staff it, he invited scholars from all over the world. Euclid, the famous Greek mathematician, came from Athens to head the new mathematics department.

The Alexandrian school was almost seven hundred years old when Hypatia was born in A.D. 370. By the time of her birth, Greece had been invaded by Roman armies many times and was no longer the power it had once been. Alexandria itself had fallen completely under the control of the Romans. As the Roman war machine expanded, it had adopted techniques that it found useful for its expansion. Greek mathematics, not useful in this way, was neither appreciated or encouraged. Actually the Romans were poor mathematicians. Even arithmetic as we now know it was impossible using clumsy Roman numerals. In this hostile atmosphere, scholars fought to preserve the Greek traditions of creative inquiry. Hypatia is considered one of the last of the great teachers involved in this struggle.

Life and Death

Much of Hypatia's life is clouded in legend. We know she was the daughter of a mathematician. Her father was Theon, a noted mathematician and astronomer. It is thought that she never married. She was probably educated by her father. Some accounts tell that her father guided every aspect of her education. In order to develop this most "perfect human being" he supervised the improvement of her body as well as her mind. Exercises of all kinds were a regular part of each day. The rigorous training apparently achieved its objective: her beauty and talents were legendary. She was one of the university's most popular lecturers. Students came from Europe, Asia, and Africa to hear her lectures on the works of Diophantus and others. She was greatly admired as a magnificent teacher and human being, almost as an oracle.

As a pagan, Hypatia was in a dangerous position in the Alexandria of her time. Although the new Christianity was developing and spreading, Hypatia remained loyal to her Greek religious beliefs. The Christians were hostile to these pagan ideas, regarding them as the cause of the gradual weakening of Roman character. Many actually believed that the decline of the Empire largely resulted from these pagan influences. Continually pressed and attacked by barbarians from the north, the Roman Empire was finding it more and more difficult to protect itself from that direction. So it was not surprising that the pagan Greeks in Alexandria became a scapegoat for the growing frustrations of the Romans. During one of the periodic outbreaks of hostility, Hypatia was brutally murdered by an Alexandrian mob.

Some historians believe that Hypatia was the victim of a power struggle between two Alexandrian leaders. Orestes, the Roman prefect of Egypt, had long been her friend and protector. Cyril, who became patriarch of Alexandria in 412 A.D., was committed to eliminating all heretical beliefs in order to strengthen Christianity. Hypatia, as an outspoken supporter of Greek scientific rational thought, could not be tolerated. Popular as she was, she was to find Cyril a dangerous opponent. Even Orestes could not protect her from the mob which had been enflamed against her by Cyril.

Several lurid accounts of Hypatia's death have come down to us. One particularly exotic one suggests that her flesh was scraped from her bones with oyster shells. In the mid-nineteenth century, the English writer Charles Kingsley wrote a fictionalized account of her life. He writes that although a plot against her had been suspected, her servants could not believe she was in any real danger. They knew for certain their mistress could turn aside lightning. "The very wild beasts would not tear her, if she were thrown into the amphitheatre."[1] In a typically Victorian description of her murder, which he sets in a Christian church, "domed, candles, incense, blazing altar", he writes . . . "with one hand she clasped her golden locks around her, the other long white arm was stretched upward toward the great still Christ, appealing, from man to God . . . Then wail on wail, long, wild, ear-piercing, rang along the vaulted roofs . . . then finally shrieks died into moans, and moans into silence. Burn the bones to ashes! Scatter them into the sea!"[2] Twenty years after Hypatia's death, philosophy in Alexandria was flickering down to the very socket. Her murder was its deathblow. Her murder was the end of the Platonic succession.

Indeed, Hypatia's death marks the end of the great age of Greek mathematics. In 641, just a few hundred years later, Alexandria was invaded and destroyed by the Arabs. In this way the thousand years of dominance of the Alexandrian school ended, and Western mathematics went into a dormant period lasting also a thousand years.

Ancient Alexandria: View of the harbor. At the time Hypatia lived there, Alexandria was a major center of Greek intellectual life.

The years most historians attribute to Hypatia are concealed in the number puzzle below. Can you discover what they are?

The year of Hypatia's birth is a three-digit number.
The third digit is the additive identity.*
The first two digits are the twelfth prime number.** (Remember, 2 is the first prime number; 1 is *not* considered a prime number.)

____ ____ ____

The year of Hypatia's death is also a three-digit number.
The first two digits are the thirteenth prime number.
The third digit is the third prime number.

____ ____ ____

---

* See Appendix 9 for definition of additive identity.
**See page 3 for definition of prime number.

Hypatia's Work

We know very little, for certain, about Hypatia's work. No copies of anything she has written exist today. It is believed that she was primarily an algebraist inspired by Diophantus, an important mathematician who lived and worked in Alexandria shortly before her time. We know that Hypatia wrote a commentary on Diophantus' *Arithmetica*. Much of what we actually know about her work comes from the letters of one of her pupils, Synesius of Cyrene, later Bishop of Ptolemais. Some of these letters are said to contain instructions by Hypatia on how to build a number of scientific instruments. One such instrument is an astrolabe, a device for measuring the positions of the stars and planets. These references suggest that Hypatia probably lectured on simple mechanics as well as mathematics, philosophy, and astronomy.

Hypatia also wrote *On the Conics of Apollonius*, a book about the work of a prominent Alexandrian who lived five hundred years before. Here she seemed to be aware of the importance of the conic sections, curves which had so fascinated her Greek ancestors. Later, at the beginning of the seventeenth century, the mathematics of the conic sections were to become extremely important. With the birth of modern science came the discovery that many natural phenomena could best be described by curves which were conic sections. The Greeks had known nothing of this. They had merely been intrigued by the fascinating relationships among the conic sections. A circle, an ellipse, a parabola, a hyperbola—all these figures could be formed by passing a plane through a single cone. As the position of this intersecting plane varied, the intersection took on the different shapes.

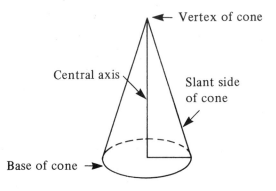

Vertex of cone

Central axis

Slant side of cone

Base of cone

The Concept of Conic Sections

Try to imagine cutting through a cone with a great flat knife. Hold the knife parallel to the base of the cone. Can you see that the resulting cut will be a circle?

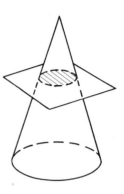

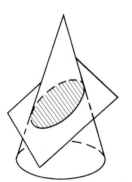

Imagine the cone intact again. Cut through it again, this time with the knife slanted somewhat. Can you see that now the cut will look like an ellipse?

Imagine the cone whole again. This time start the knife somewhere at one slant side, and hold it at an angle, parallel to the opposite slant side. Keeping the slant of the knife constant, cut down to the base of the cone. The curve that will appear on the cone is called a *parabola*.

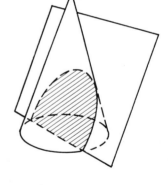

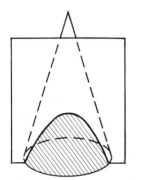

Last, cut through the cone parallel to the line coming up through the center of the cone, the central axis. Start cutting at the slant of the cone; keep the knife parallel to this central axis. The shape of this cut is a *hyperbola*.

To make certain that these concepts are clear, trace or cut out figures A, B, C, D, and E on pages 15 and 17. Use these models in completing the sentences on page 19.

Make a Model

Cut out the following figures. Tape each figure so that the cross-hatched strip is under the opposite slant edge—*a* to *a*, *b* to *b*. Figure 2-1 will be a cone. Figures 2-2, 2-3, 2-4, and 2-5 will show how cone A will look after being cut by planes at different angles. See page 17.

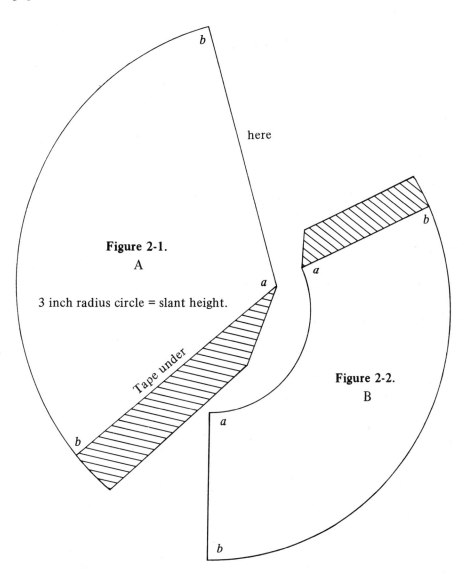

b

here

Figure 2-1.
A

3 inch radius circle = slant height.

a

a   *a*

b

Tape under

b

Figure 2-2.
B

a

b

Can you tell which conic section is represented by each figure?

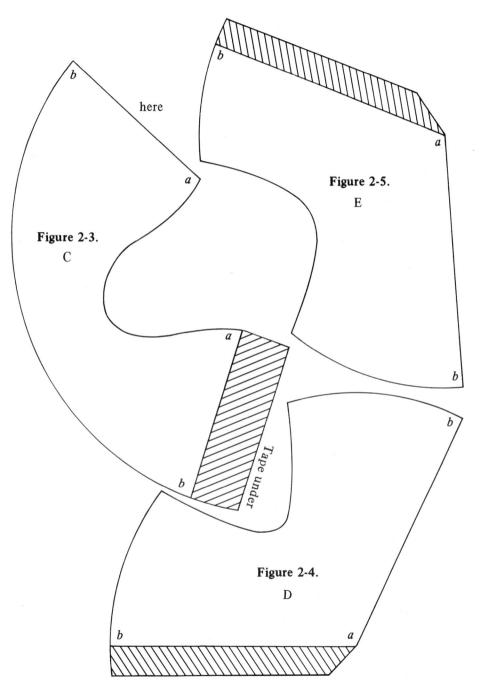

b

here

a

Figure 2-3.

C

b

a

Figure 2-5.

E

a

b

a

Tape under

b

b

Figure 2-4.

D

b

a

To differentiate Figures 2-4 and 2-5, look at the completed figures from the side. Remember, the hyperbola is formed by a planar cut parallel to the central axis of the cone.

Clear So Far?

This plane cuts the cone parallel to the cone's _____. The figure formed by this cut is a _____.

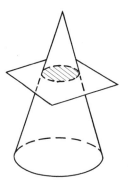

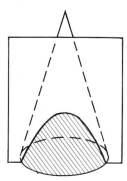

This plane cuts the cone parallel to the central axis of the cone. The figure formed by this cut is a _____.

This plane is cutting through the cone at a slant. The figure formed is a _____.

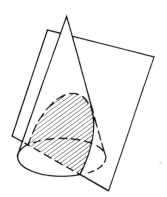

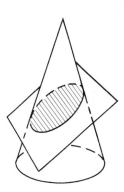

This plane is cutting through the cone parallel with the slant height of the cone. The figure formed by this cut is a _____.

Suppose lines A, B, C, and D represent edges of planes perpendicular to this page. Suppose all these planes are cutting through this cone. The shapes of the resulting cuts will be:

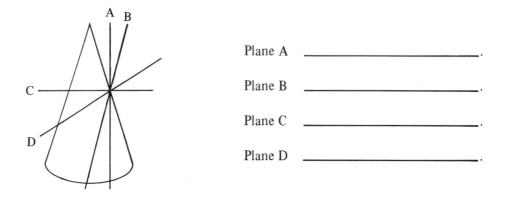

Plane A _____.

Plane B _____.

Plane C _____.

Plane D _____.

Another Way: The Conic as a Path of Points

We may also describe conic sections as loci or paths of points. Each type of curve can then be described by its own formula or rule of formation. The description of a circle is well known: the path of all points the same distance from a particular point. The *center* of the circle is the point from which all the points *on* the circle are equally distant. The constant distance from this center is called the *radius* of the circle.

The activities on the following pages will generate paths of points of other conic sections: parabolas, ellipses, and hyperbolas. The background circles used in the following activities are called *concentric* circles. *Concentric circles* share the same center point but have different radii.

Notice also that the radii of the concentric circles in these diagrams increase by a *fixed* amount. (Some diagrams contain only parts of circles because of space limitations.)

The Parabola

A *parabola* is the path of all points which are the same distance from a fixed point (the focus) and a fixed line. In Figure 2-6 the *fixed point* is F, the center of the concentric circles. The *fixed line* is *line O*, one of several parallel horizontal lines in Figure 2-6.

Points A_1 and A_2 are points where circle 2 intersects line 2. These points will be on the parabola since they satisfy the definition above.

$A_1F = A_2F =$ _____ units.

Points A_1 and A_2 are each _____ units from F.

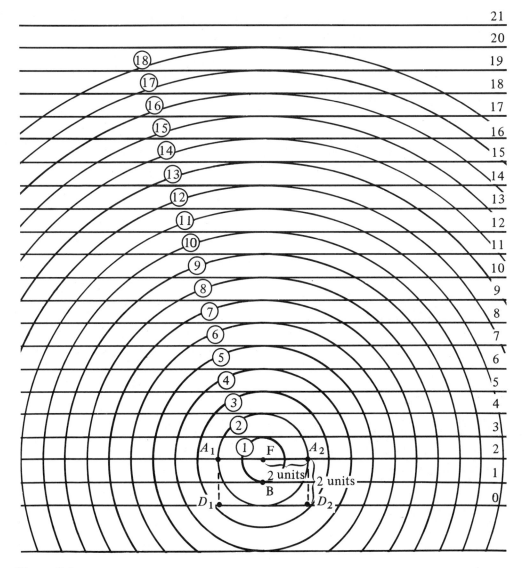

Figure 2-6.

Also, $A_1D_1 = A_2D_2 =$ _____ units. (This is true since the horizontal lines in the figures are _____ units apart.)

Therefore points A_1 and A_2 satisfy the definition of points on a parabola; they are the same distance from both fixed point F and fixed line O.

B will also be on the parabolic curve, since B is the intersection of circle 1 and line 1. B is also the same distance from both F and line O.

B is _____ unit from both point F and line O.

Mark the intersections of circle 3 with line 3.

These points will be _____ units from both center point F and line O.

Continue marking the intersections of circles and lines which share the same number. These intersection points will be equally distant from point F and line O.

How many points will the intersection of each circle and line produce? _____.

When you have located as many sets of points as there are intersecting circles and lines, connect these points with a smooth curve.

The curve you will have produced is called a _____.

The Ellipse

An *ellipse* is the path of points whose total distances from two fixed points are equal.

Figure 2-7 consists of *two* sets of _____ circles.

Here, as before, each circle has a radius that exceeds the one immediately inside it

by _____ unit.

The point which marks the center of one circle is labeled _____.   The point

which marks the center of the second circle is labeled _____.

The oval figure you see on these circles is called an _____.

Notice point S on this figure. This point is where two circles cross. Such a point is

called an intersection.

The circles that intersect at point S are labeled ② and ⑦ .

All points on circle ② are _____ units from center F_1.

Therefore line F_1S is _____ units long.

All points on circle ⑦ are _____ units from center F_2.

Therefore line F_2S is _____ units long.

Notice then that $F_1S + F_2S = 2+7=9$.

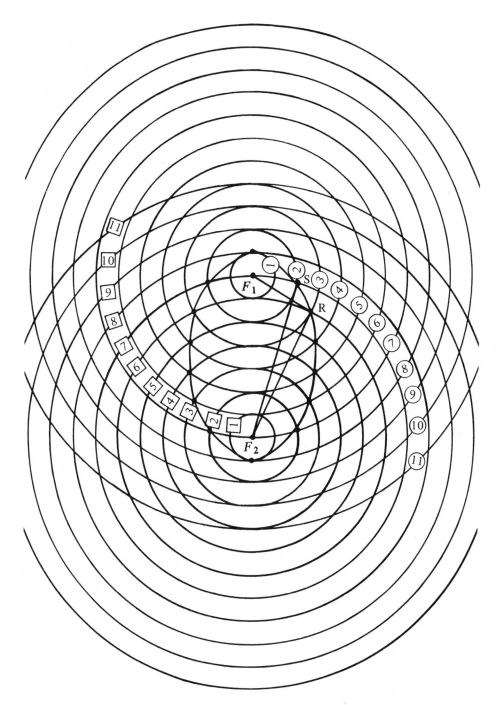

Figure 2-7.

Look at point R on the ellipse. This point is the _____

of circles ◯ and ☐ .

$F_1R + F_2R =$ _____ + _____ units.

Notice that all the points on this ellipse are on the intersections of two circles, the sum of whose radii add up to 9. Choose another point on the ellipse. Check this relation.

Find the ellipse formed by the intersections of circles whose radii add up to 8 units. (Note: ⑥ + [2] gives a different point from ② + [6] .)

The Hyperbola

A *hyperbola* is the path of points whose distances from two fixed points have **equal differences**. Remember, in Figure 2-7 each point on the ellipse was a total of 9 units from F_1 and F_2. That is, $F_1P + F_2P = 9$.

A point on a hyperbola would be one for which $F_1P - F_2P =$ some constant number.

Figure 2-8 is again made up of _____ circles.

The center of one set is at point _____ . The center of the second set is at

point _____ .

In the example below, the hyperbola consists of the set of points whose difference is 3. ($F_1H_1 - F_2H_1 = 3$.) Notice points H_1, H_2, H_3, H_4, and H_5. Point H_1 is the intersection of ③ and [6] .

③ is _____ units from F_1.

[6] is _____ units from F_2.

Therefore $6 - 3 = 3$ units is a point on the hyperbola.

Check some other points on this curve. You will find that all the differences are equal to 3 units.

On this same diagram locate the set of points whose difference of distance is 5 units. This is the hyperbola where $F_1P - F_2P = 5$. The coordinates of these points will be solutions to the equation ☐ − ◯ = 5. For example [8] − ③ = 5; therefore the intersection of circles [8] and ③ will be a point on the hyperbola.

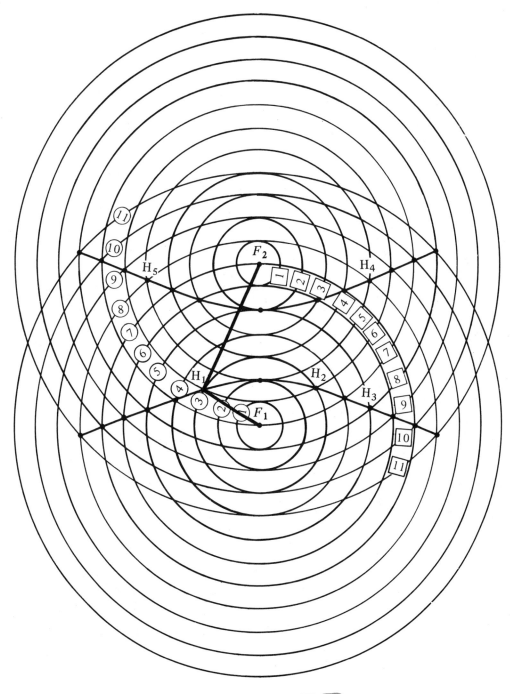

Figure 2-8.

Parabolic antennae reflect incoming parallel radio or TV waves at one point, the focus, at which the receiver is located.

Applications of the hyperbola.

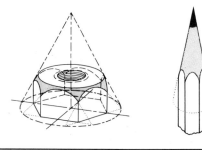

Basic particles of matter, the electrons, travel in circular and elliptical paths about the nucleus of the atom.

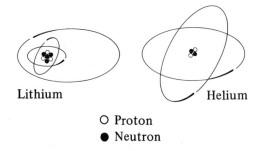

Lithium   Helium

○ Proton
● Neutron

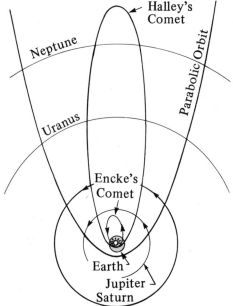

The elliptical orbit of Halley's Comet and the smaller ellipse of Encke's Comet. An imaginary parabolic orbit is also indicated, extending out of the drawing to infinity.

Figure 2-9. Some applications of parabolas, hyperbolas, and ellipses.

Hypatia and the Arithmetica of Diophantus

Hypatia's commentaries on the work of Diophantus did not survive the many hundreds of years between the time of its writing and the present. However, historians agree that Hypatia *did* write such a work, and that it was important.

Diophantus is often called the leading algebraist of antiquity. He is thought to have lived and taught in Alexandria shortly before Hypatia did. Diophantine equations are named after him. They are equations whose solutions have been restricted to integers.

Consider various ways to make change for a dollar using nickels, dimes, and quarters. When you solve such a problem you are solving a diophantine equation.

An equation which expresses this is $5n + 10d + 25q = 100$, where n is the number of nickels, d is the number of dimes, and q is the number of quarters.

Fill in Table 2-1 below. Solve the diophantine equation. How many different solutions can you find? How many solutions using only two kinds of coins? How many solutions using three kinds of coins?

Table 2-1

n = nickels (how many?)	d = dimes (how many?)	q = quarters (how many?)	Dollar Bill = $5n + 10d + 25q = 100$
2	4	2	$(5 \cdot 2)+(10 \cdot 4)+(25 \cdot 2) = 100$
1	—	3	$(5 \cdot 1)+(10 \cdot \_)+(25 \cdot 3) = 100$
5	5	—	$(5 \cdot 5)+(10 \cdot 5)+(25 \cdot \_) = 100$
—	—	—	$(5 \cdot \_)+(10 \cdot \_)+(25 \cdot \_) = 100$
.	.	.	.
.	.	.	.
.	.	.	.

Emilie du Châtelet 1706–1749

Within a century of Hypatia's death, Rome itself was conquered by barbarians. For more than a thousand years afterward, nothing significantly new happened in mathematics or science in the West. And then, toward the end of the Middle Ages, the situation began to change. Copernicus and Kepler developed important new theories describing the motion of the planets. Not long after, Galileo, experimenting with falling bodies and projectiles on earth, made new observations about the forces acting on them. Then finally, in the seventeenth century, Isaac Newton synthesized these new ideas in the *Principia*, a major work which marks the dawn of modern science. Shortly after this, in a time historians call the Enlightenment, Emilie du Châtelet lived and worked.

Her full name was Gabrielle-Emilie Le Tonnelier de Breteuil, Marquise du Châtelet-Lomont, and she was born in France in 1706. As a beautiful, wealthy aristocrat, she might easily have lived her life immersed in the superficial pleasures of the French salons. Instead she became an active participant in the events which were making the Enlightenment an exciting period. This was not in itself surprising, for fashionable women of the French upper classes were expected to be clever as well as attractive. However, the depth of her intellect and her original contributions to what was happening around her were unusual. This was even more exceptional at a time when, for the typical aristocratic Frenchwoman, education meant being sent to a convent at age five and being fetched out about ten years later for a suitable marriage.

During the time that Emilie du Châtelet lived, France was a haven for letter writers. At least in the group of which she was a part, people corresponded voluminously. Even people living in the same house sometimes carried on elaborate correspondences. Drawing heavily on the letters of the period, Samuel Edwards has written a delightful book about Emilie du Châtelet and her relationship with Voltaire, the eighteenth-century poet, historian, and philosopher. This book, *The Divine Mistress*, conveys a marvelous picture of Emilie du Châtelet. Perhaps much of what Edwards writes should be taken with reservation but the letters seem to speak for themselves. Edwards begins his book with a witty testimonial to Emilie by Voltaire.

Emilie, in truth, is the divine mistress, endowed with beauty, wit, compassion and all of the other womanly virtues. Yet I frequently wish she were less learned and her mind less sharp, that her appetites for the making of love were less voracious, and more than all else, that she would acquire both the ability and desire to hold her tongue on occasion. [1]

The Child: a Pessimistic Prognosis

Emilie's father's letters, describing her as a child, are hilarious. Her father was a royal courtier. His full name and titles are awesome: Louis-Nicolas Le Tonnelier de Breteuil, Baron of Preuilly and chief of protocol at the court. Perhaps her parents' attitude toward Emilie as a young child is a clue to her unusual development. "By the time Emilie was seven or eight," writes Edwards, "it appeared that of all the children she alone had been deprived of her mother's good looks." [2]

> *"My youngest," Louis-Nicolas wrote sadly, "is an odd creature destined to become the homeliest of women. Were it not for the low opinion I hold of several bishops, I would prepare her for a religious life and let her hide in a convent. She stands as tall as a girl twice her years, she has prodigious strength, like that of a wood-cutter, and is clumsy beyond belief. Her feet are huge, but one forgets them the moment one notices her enormous hands. Her skin, alas, is as rough as a nutmeg grater, and altogether she is as ugly as a Gascon peasant recruit in the royal footguards." [3]*

Emilie was unusually tall—almost five feet nine inches, an exceptional height even for men at that time. (She was nearly a head taller than Voltaire.) Because of her height and appearance the family felt that Emilie would never find a husband and had best be prepared to spend her life as a spinster. So from the age of six or seven she was surrounded with unusually fine tutors and governesses. Since she was ignored by almost all her relatives, her best chance of receiving adult attention was to please her tutors. This she could do best by being a fine student. And so she was.

In an effort to cure Emily's clumsiness her father also made her into a superb horsewoman, and it is said that she could beat most gentlemen of the court in a duel.

The Woman—Surprise!

Despite the pessimistic outlook for the young child, by her fifteenth year Emilie had suddenly matured into a surprising beauty. The foundations for her future as a scholar had already been established, however. And beauty and intelligence were to combine in Emilie to produce a fascinating woman. She was a strong person who knew what she was about and enjoyed a great deal of control over her own life.

When she was almost nineteen Emilie cooly evaluated her marriage prospects and made her plan. Her dowry would be small, she reasoned, so a brilliant marriage was essentially impossible. With great care, she decided what attributes she wanted in a husband, and then set about finding him. The husband she was looking for should be older and therefore less likely to interfere in her life. He should be of higher rank than her father. (Emilie liked the idea of moving up in the world.) And he had best be someone who would be flattered by acquiring a wife who was brainy as well as beautiful.

The Marquis Florent-Claude du Châtelet-Lomont fit Emilie's requirements beautifully. He had an impressive background and owned a number of large estates. He was older than Emilie by some 10 years. An up-and-coming officer, he was an honest, direct, pleasure-loving man who had decided that he needed a wife because he needed an heir. He didn't have much cash, so his estates were run-down—but he wasn't much concerned about marrying for money either. Emilie dressed splendidly for their first introduction. All her life she was to have a passion for expensive and beautiful clothes. Florent-Claude was impressed. Besides, says Edwards, "he was just shrewd enough to realize that someone as tall as she would give birth to large children."[4] Edwards describes the letters of other courtiers as they observed the courtship: "The Marquis talked about nothing but his campaigns, Emilie discussed only her evolving metaphysical philosophical concepts, and neither understood or cared to understand a word the other said."[5] In a way, that was the essence of their marriage. Both got from it exactly what they wanted. It was a fine arrangement.

The Young Matron

Socially, Emilie was much freer as a married woman than she could ever have been unmarried. She was a good wife in the way her husband most required. She produced his heir without too much fuss. During the first years of their marriage she gave birth to two children, first a girl and then the boy. When she was 27 a second son was born, but he lived only a short while. As a mother Emilie was probably no better or worse than most women of her class. She saw her children briefly each day, but they were raised mainly by nurses and governesses.

During these years the Marquis was often away with his troops, while Emilie was heavily involved in the life at court. She loved the social whirl, the gambling, and the company of powerful men. She never neglected her mathematical studies, however. Her position allowed her to obtain the services of some important mathematicians as teachers, and she was becoming a fine mathematician herself.

Determined not to be a slave to convention, Emilie once went to a cafe that was restricted to men. It was a gathering place for scientists and mathematicians who were her colleagues and friends. She was turned away the first time, only to return dressed as a man and be admitted.

PRINCIPES
MATHÉMATIQUES

DE LA

PHILOSOPHIE NATURELLE,

Par feue Madame la Marquise DU CHASTELLET.

TOME PREMIER.

A PARIS,

Chez {
DESAINT & SAILLANT, rue S. Jean de Beauvais.
ET
LAMBERT, rue & à côté de la Comédie Françoise,
au Parnasse.
}

PRÉFACE HISTORIQUE.

CETTE traduction que les plus savans Hommes de France devoient faire, & que les autres doivent étudier, une femme l'a entreprise & achevée à l'étonnement & à la gloire de son pays. Gabrielle-Emilie de Breteuil, Marquise du Châtelet, est l'Auteur de cette Traduction, devenue nécessaire à tous

HISTORICAL PREFACE

This translation which the most learned Men of France should have done, and which others should study, a woman has undertaken and achieved to the astonishment and to the glory of her country. Gabrielle-Emilie de Breteuil, Marquise du Châtelet, is the author . . .

Shown at top is the title page of du Châtelet's translation of Newton's *Principia*. At bottom is the beginning of the preface, written by Voltaire.

After the birth of her first child Emilie started to become personally involved in the extramarital alliances which were fairly common at that time. Rules then were quite different than they are today, but the contemporary standards were taken seriously and strictly adhered to in "good society." Men were allowed any number of mistresses. It was considered poor taste, however, for a woman to have more than one lover at a time. And so according to the customs of her time Emilie became a fashionable woman of the world.

An Alliance for a Lady

The details of du Châtelet's meetings and life with Voltaire fill books. We shall try to include only enough details of their relationship to illuminate Emilie herself.

Voltaire was nearing 40 when their affair began. He was already considered one of the most important figures in eighteenth-century Europe. In one sense, Voltaire and Emilie seemed completely unsuited to one another. Voltaire, always in delicate health, had frequent stomach disorders and needed careful rest and diet. Emilie, on the other hand, was superbly healthy and overwhelmingly energetic. She normally slept two to four hours a night and felt that she could manage with even less.

Although he was very popular, Voltaire was often on the verge of arrest because of his writings. His frequent attacks on the French monarchy with its lack of respect for personal liberties brought him into periodic conflict with authority. Cirey, one of the country estates of Emilie's husband, was close to the Belgian border and seemed an ideal retreat when such an incident occurred. With Voltaire's money and Emilie's expertise in redoing houses, the two decided to escape there, restore the house, and live happily ever after, far from the distractions and dangers of Paris.

Stories of the restoration of the Chateau de Cirey are most amusing. In a letter to Mme de la Neuville, Voltaire wrote "Mme. du Châtelet is going to put windows where I have put doors. She is changing staircases into chimneys and chimneys into staircases. Where I have instructed the workmen to construct a library, she tells them to place a salon. My salon she will make into a bath closet. She is going to plant lime trees where I have proposed to place elms, and where I have planted herbs and vegetables (at last, my own kitchen gardens, and I was already taking great pride in them!), nothing will make her happy but a flower bed."[6] The two settled down at Cirey to what were to be 15 years together before Emilie's death.

Emilie's husband knew of her association with Voltaire. However, his attitude toward their relationship was common for those days: he ignored it. From time to time, when convenient, he himself lived briefly at Cirey. Actually, he and Voltaire liked and respected each other, and enjoyed long walks together when Florent-Claude was there. Most of the time, however, he was off pursuing his own career and enjoying his adventures as an officer to the king.

Both Emilie and Voltaire worked hard during this time. Even when they entertained house guests, which they loved to do, it was understood that the guests were to amuse themselves most of the day, while Emilie and Voltaire worked. Later, work would stop and everyone would gather for entertainment and amusements. A favorite pastime at Cirey was producing amateur theatricals written by Voltaire, in which everyone would take part. Emilie loved to act. When there were no guests at Cirey, Emilie and Voltaire would often work continually, Emilie still sleeping only a few hours at night.

Much has been written about Emilie's effect on Voltaire and his thinking. There is no doubt that their relationship was important to both of them. Both Emilie and Voltaire were prolific workers.

Emilie, the Savant

As Emilie progressed as a scholar, she began to publish and acquire an impressive reputation. Her aristocratic contemporaries refused to take her seriously, however. They felt that the flighty, notorious, jewel-loving Mme. du Chatelet was just showing off again. But according to Edwards, du Chatelet was indifferent to their opinions. She knew her own worth as a mathematician, scientist, classicist, and translator, and she knew she was respected by her peers in these fields. Although she cared very much about how she was perceived in both worlds, she had the good sense not to confuse the two of them. "She no more expected a philosopher or a physicist to admire a new gown than she looked for the applause of the salon habitués when she published a new book."[7] Frederick the Great, ruler of Prussia, who admired Voltaire and over many years attempted to attract him away from France and Emilie, wrote to congratulate her on a published work. "Without wishing to flatter you," he wrote her, "I can assure you that I should never have believed your sex, usually so delightfully gifted with all the graces, capable also of such deep knowledge, minute research and solid discovery as appears in your fine work."[8]

By 1747, young scientists and mathematicians began to appear at Cirey to study with Emilie. It was a great personal achievement that such people should have voluntarily sought a woman as a teacher.

A Woman's Death

Emilie worked seriously in mathematics until the day she died. Her life ended suddenly in 1749. She died of childbed fever after the birth of her fourth child, the result of a love affair with a much younger man. Emilie worked until the very moment the baby was born. Hamel, in his book *An Eighteenth Century Marquise*, describes the birth: "It appeared that when the little girl was born, its mother was at her writing-desk, scribbling some Newtonian theories. The child was laid temporarily on a quarto volume of geometry. The mother was taken straight to bed."[9]

Recovery seemed normal after the birth. The people Emilie cared most about gathered round, sharing her company as she became stronger. Edwards writes that her room was often crowded with visitors. Suddenly, with no prior warning, she was dead! Such unexpected deaths from childbed fever were not uncommon among new mothers at that time. What is even more tragic, though, is that the baby girl also died just a few days after her mother.

In her book *Women in Mathematics*, Lynn Osen points out that although Emilie du Châtelet's family soon vanished (her first son lived to manhood but was killed on the guillotine, and her grandson died during the French Revolution), her works live on. Of these, her translation and commentaries on Newton's *Principia* are considered particularly important. This work, which did not appear in final print until 1759, after her death, remains to this day the only French translation of the work.

Emilie du Châtelet lived during the period known as the Enlightenment. Can you remember the years of her birth and death?

The year of her death is a four-digit number.
The first two digits are the seventh prime number. (Remember that 1 is not considered a prime number. 2 is the first prime number.)
The last two digits are the square of the fourth prime number.
The number of years she lived was the same as the fourteenth prime number.

Emilie du Châtelet lived from ___ ___ ___ ___ to ___ ___ ___ ___.

Emilie du Châletet's Work

Some of the women in this book made important original contributions to mathematics. Others were expositors rather than creative mathematicians. Emilie du Châtelet was one of the latter. The work for which she is best known is her translation and analysis of Newton's masterpiece, the *Principia*.

The powerful Newtonian scientific method caught the imaginations of intellectuals during the Enlightenment. They thought that perhaps, by applying the new scientific method, laws could be discovered to help people understand social forces in the same way that physical forces were becoming understood. Embedded in the ideas science brought to philosophy seemed to be the assumption that no limits existed to what humanity could understand and achieve; people had free will and could control their own future. Scientific determinism was another part of these ideas. Scientists believed that if one were able to describe an event completely (by some formula), then by knowing the state of the system at any particular instant one would know it at any future time. Some thought, that this too might have important implications beyond science. Emilie du Châtelet's translation and analysis of the *Principia* was important in spreading these ideas from England to the Continent in the mid-eighteenth century. To appreciate the importance of what she did, then, it is necessary first to get some feeling for the monumental importance of Newton's *Principia*, where these methods seemed to yield such powerful results.

The Birth of Modern Science

For some time before Newton had lived, the scientific method as we now understand it was being developed by such scientists as Galileo and Kepler. The ancient Greeks had tried to understand nature by deductive reasoning, a method which seemed to work very well in mathematics. However, Galileo and others began to challenge this approach. For example, instead of assuming logically and intuitively that heavier objects fall faster than lighter ones, as had the Greeks, they began doing experiments and recording the results of what they saw. Often they found that what they had expected did not in fact happen. So instead of drawing conclusions from logical deduction alone, they continued doing experiments. From the data collected in this way, they would try to induce a pattern or formula with which to **predict** further experimental results. This is called **induction**; it is the basis of the modern scientific method. As a method, it was to prove extremely powerful.

Using inductive methods, Kepler discovered that the planets move around the sun in elliptical orbits, rather than in orbits based on circles as had been believed before. A little later, Galileo's experiments with falling bodies on earth showed that the time required for an object to fall to earth depended only on its height, and had no relation to its mass. (This was an exciting new idea: earlier belief had intuitively assumed that heavier objects fell faster than lighter ones.) Galileo also developed techniques to measure the mysterious force which made objects fall *down* rather than in any other direction. Newton's great contribution was the realization that the force that Galileo was measuring and the force keeping Kepler's planets moving on their elliptic orbits instead of flying off into space were one and the same. These ideas, formalized in the *Principia* as the theory of universal gravitation, had the great effect of unifying seemingly unrelated events. Newton's single set of laws—the laws of motion—predicted the behavior of both Kepler's planets and Galileo's falling objects.

Calculus—The Powerful Tool

Analysis of these new concepts required a new mathematics. Mathematical tools were needed that could deal with changing speed (acceleration) and other processes which had never been described precisely before. Approximation methods had been developed and were being used long before, first by the Greeks and later by others. Kepler, in his work, was already using many of the concepts we now call integral calculus. However seventy-odd years were to elapse before Newton and Leibniz, working independently in different places, finally gave definitive form to the calculus as we know it today. This was the mathematics Newton needed in order to develop his ideas in the *Principia*. This mathematics could deal directly with the ideas of motion, with instantaneous rates of change, which were so important to the growth of modern science. In order to do this, calculus introduced two new operations into mathematics. These operations are called *differentiation* and *integration.*

Arithmetic operations $(+, -, \times, \div)$ operate on *numbers*.

The operations of the *calculus* (differentiation and integration) operate on *functions.*

Arithmetic Operation Power (An exercise and amusement)

Using the digits from the date of Du Châtelet's death, 1749, generate as many numbers as possible by using simple arithmetic operations, in any order, to combine the 1, 7, 4, and 9.

For example: $(7+4)-(9+1)=1$

$\qquad\qquad\quad (4 \times 1)-(9-7)=2.$

Can you show 3? 4? How many others?

What is a function?

A function is **a rule which relates two or more variables**. Given one value, the function rule provides a means of obtaining a related value. This concept is taught to elementary school students these days using the function machine model.

Look at the examples in Figures 3-1 and 3-2. Make sure you understand them before you go on. The function machine is a model to help students understand the concept of a function. Here a value becomes input for the machine. Inside the machine the function rule is applied to the value. The output of the machine is the "transformed" value. This is not a formal definition of the process, but these examples should make the process intuitively clear.

Function Machine Problems

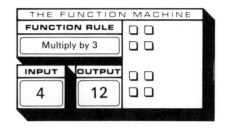

Think about the function machine and give the missing
number or rule.

1. Function Rule

Input	Output
2	6
9	27
A 8	||||||
B 5	||||||
C 7	||||||

Multiply by 3

2. Function Rule

Multiply by 4

Input	Output
2	8
A 4	||||||
B 9	||||||
C 6	||||||
D 8	||||||

3. Function Rule

Multiply by 5

Input	Output
A 3	||||||
B 7	||||||
9	45
C 6	||||||
D 8	||||||

4. Function Rule

A ||||||||||||||||||||

Input	Output
2	10
3	15
7	35
B 6	||||||
C ||||||	20

★5. Function Rule

Multiply by 2

Input	Output
2	4
A 5	||||||
B ||||||	8
C ||||||	14
D ||||||	12

★6. Function Rule

A ||||||||||||||||||||

Input	Output
2	4
3	9
5	25
B 4	||||||
C 1	||||||

Figure 3-1.

The Function Machine

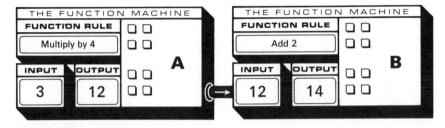

Function machine A is connected to function machine B. The output number from machine A becomes the input number for machine B. We put in 3. Machine A operates. Machine B operates. We get 14.

Think about connected function machines and give the numbers and words you think should go in the gray spaces.

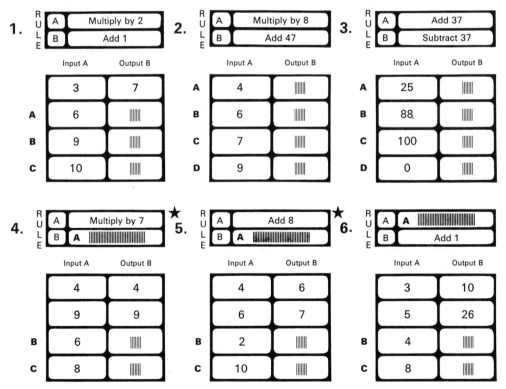

Figure 3-2.

More Complicated Examples

Figures 3-1 and 3-2 are examples of simple function machines. Sometimes a function may describe a more complicated situation. For example, Galileo discovered that for a freely falling body, the distance fallen is related to the time it has been falling. The formula $d = 16 t^2$ tells about the relationship. This function relates distance in feet (d) to time in seconds (t) in a way that describes all freely falling bodies. Given any time t, a distance d can be found.

Complete Table 3-1. See how this more complicated function behaves.

Table 3-1.

Time	$t^2 = t \times t$	$16\, t^2 = d$ (distance)
1	$1 \times 1 = 1$	$16 \times 1 = 16$
2	$2 \times 2 = 4$	$16 \times 4 = 64$
3	_____	_____
4	_____	_____
5	_____	_____
6	_____	_____
7	_____	_____
.		
.		
.		

Look at the values of d in Table 3-1.

In 1 second, the object has fallen _____ feet.

In 2 seconds, the object has fallen _____ feet.

In 3 seconds, the object has falled _____ feet.

The object seems to be falling at different speeds, faster and faster, as it approaches the ground. Suppose one asked how fast the object was falling at any particular *instant* during its fall. That's a question the calculus can help to answer! Such a question would have been impossible to answer before the development of the calculus. By operating on the function $d = 16t^2$, the calculus comes up with another function which describes exactly how fast the object is moving at any particular moment in time. The operation which does this is called *differentiation*.

Function and Rate of Change

This next example may give a better idea of a *function* which describes the *rate of change* of one element with respect to another.

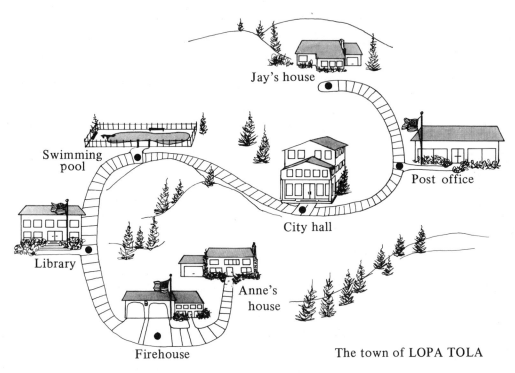

Figure 3-3.

Figure 3-3.

Constant Change

Anne is walking her dog Tico. Figure 3-3 shows their route. They walk at constant speed from Anne's house past several landmarks in the town of Lopa Tola, to Jay's house.

They are walking at 3 miles per hour. Look at the diagram in Figure 3-4. See if you understand it. Answer the questions.

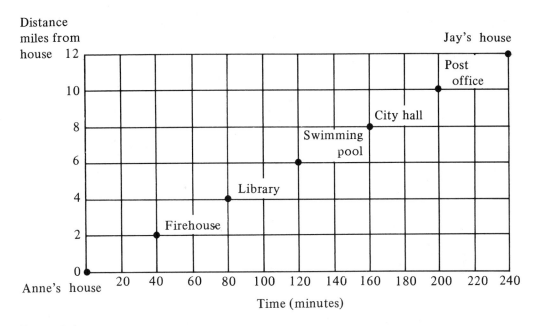

Figure 3-4.

Figure 3-4 shows the relationship between two elements or variables. .

One variable is _____.

The second variable is _____.

Use the diagram to answer the following questions.

How far is the post office from Anne's house?_____

How far is the swimming pool from Jay's house?_____

How long did it take Anne and Tico to walk from the library to the post office?

_____

How long did it take to walk from the firehouse to the swimming pool?

_____

If it took t minutes to walk d miles, we say that the rate, or velocity, of the walk was $d \div t$ miles per minute.

Since the distance from the firehouse to the swimming pool was _____ miles, and Anne and Tico walked this distance in _____ minutes, Anne and Tico's velocity while walking from the firehouse to the swimming pool was _____ .

Fill in Table 3-2, which shows the distance-time relationships among all the places on the trip. What do you notice about the values of all the entries?

Table 3-2.

Distance between points / Time of walk between points	Anne's house	Fire- house	Library	Swim- ming pool	City hall	Post office	Jay's house
Anne's house	X						
Firehouse		X					
Library			X				
Swimming pool				X			
City hall					X		
Post office						X	
Jay's house							X

What was Anne and Tico's velocity on their walk?

in miles per minute? _____

in miles per hour? _____

On this journey we say that the girl and dog were walking at *constant* speed. Why do we say this?

Up to this point calculus would not be useful. Since Anne and Tico were walking at constant speed, calculus is not needed.

Nonconstant change

In the next problem we begin to see where calculus might come in handy. We still do not use it, but the problem is basically different from the one just before.

Look at Figure 3-5. Each point, *A* through *H*, still represents some information about a journey through Lopa Tola. Its position on the graph tells us two things: how far the place is from Anne's house, and the time at which Anne and Tico arrived there on their walk. Each point is also a place—in one case (*D* and *E*) two points are the *same* place.

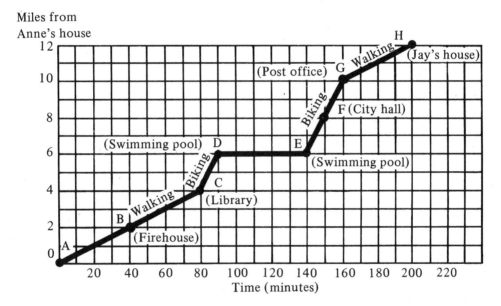

Figure 3-5.

Notice that the lines connecting the points here have different slopes (slants). This shows that Anne and Tico did not walk at constant speed over the entire trip. Some lines do not slant at all. We say that their slope is zero. Notice that *D* to *E* represents an interval during which Anne is swimming. No progress is made on the journey from Anne's house to Jay's house during this time.

Figure 3-6 charts this journey from Anne's house to Jay's house. At this point we add a new concept and a new symbol, Δ. We read Δ as "delta".

Δ*d* means *change in distance* between two points.

Δ*t* means *change in time* between two points.

Table 3-3.

Points of interest	Distance (miles) from Anne's house.	Δd (change in distance)	Time (minutes) from Anne's house	Δt (change in time)	Velocity Δd/Δt (miles/minute)
A Anne's house	0		0		
		2		40	2/40
B Firehouse	2	—	40	—	—
C Library	—	—	—	—	—
D Swimming pool	—	—	—	—	—
E Swimming pool	—	—	—	—	—
F City hall	—	—	—	—	—
G Post office	—	—	—	—	—
H Jay's house	—	—	—	—	—

Complete Table 3-3 using values from Figure 3-5. Check your results (see page 237) before going on to answer the following questions.

What is happening when $\Delta d = 0$?

List the three different values for the velocity during various parts of the journey.

————————, ————————, ————————.

Which of Anne's activities (walking, bicycling, or swimming) do these velocities represent?

The smallest value is _____. At that time, Anne is _____.

The next smallest is _____. Anne is _____.

The greatest is _____. Anne is _____.

Continuous Change

The next problem could not be solved without calculus. Look at Figure 3-6. How is it different from the preceding problems? Let us try to understand what is happening in the figure. We understand that a force has been applied on the ball when it is thrown.

Once the ball is in the air it is subjected to a combination of forces at the same time: the upward thrust of the throw and the downward force of gravity. The time that the ball is in the air—its journey up and finally down—is a result of all these forces acting on it. This can be described by a formula, but it is more complicated than any we wish to include here. So let us merely read the values on Figure 3-6 and try to understand what is happening from that.

Figure 3-6 shows the height of the ball at each point on its journey. Each point on Figure 3-6 is shown with a number pair. Remember, by convention, the first number of this pair is the measure along the horizontal coordinate—in this case, the time in seconds. The second number is the measure along the vertical coordinate—in this case, height in feet.

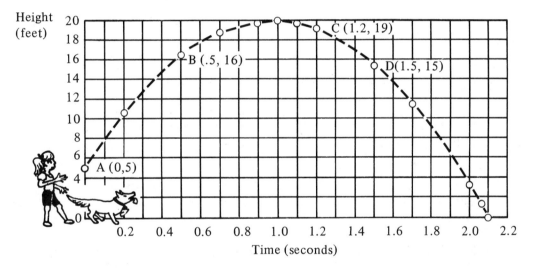

Figure 3-6. Anne threw a ball straight into the air for Tico to catch. Tico missed. The ball landed on the ground approximately 2 seconds after it left Anne's hand.

Use Figure 3-6 to answer the following questions.

What was the greatest height that the ball reached? _____

At .5 seconds (point *B*), it had reached _____ feet.

The ball started from Anne's hand, approximately _____ feet from the ground.

We say the ball traveled 16−5=11 feet in the first 0.5 seconds, or an average velocity of 11/0.5 feet/second. This is the change of distance divided by the change of time, $\Delta d/\Delta t$, over a particular interval. We can calculate the average velocity over other intervals. For example, look at the interval between C and D in Figure 3-6.

At 1.2 seconds (C) the height of the ball was _____ feet.

At 1.5 seconds (D) the height of the ball was _____ feet.

We know, therefore, that in the interval from C to D, the ball was traveling at a velocity which may be calculated as $\Delta d/\Delta t$, change of distance ÷ change of time. In this case,

Δd = _____ .

Δt = _____ .

Therefore we know that the velocity is _____ ÷ _____, or 4/.3 feet per second.

Suppose we wanted to find out the actual velocity of the ball at any particular instant. The operations of calculus can help us find that. The general idea is not hard. As before, we try to find the average velocity the ball is traveling, only now we do this over smaller and smaller intervals. We reason that we can continue doing this until the interval we are looking at, just on either side of the point we want to know about, is so small that, for our purposes, it is *no interval at all*. As we do this, we notice that the values we calculate approach closer and closer to a particular value, a "limiting value" (see below). This limiting value is the one we consider, for all practical purposes, to be the *instantaneous velocity* at any particular point we want to know about.

Karel de Leeuw, a friend and a mathematician, has a favorite example which relates differentiation and integration. Integration is the second new operation introduced by the calculus. It is the opposite of differentiation in the same way that subtraction is the opposite of addition.

Imagine driving along a straight road. At every point on the trip, you know where you are and how long it took you to get there. But your speedometer is broken. Differentiation will give you the reading which would be on the speedometer at any moment of the trip.

Suppose, on the other hand, that you are being kidnapped. You are being driven along a straight road again, but this time you cannot see the road. The only thing you can *see is the speedometer. Then, if you know the speedometer readings at any time, integration will enable you to know where you are even though you cannot see the road, since it will give you the distance you have traveled in any time* t.

Limit—a Fundamental Concept

The concept of *limit* is fundamental to both operations of the calculus, differentiation and integration.

The following puzzle (Figure 3-7, page 50) has been designed to illuminate the concept of limit.

Before you start the puzzle, think about how it looks.

How many circles do you see? _____

Since these circles share the same center we call them _____

circles.

Notice the polygons (see key concept definitions in Appendix 2) in Figure 3-7. This diagram was generated by circumscribing polygons of increasing numbers of sides on circles which, in turn, circumscribe these polygons.

Notice also that each polygon and circle contains a letter of the alphabet. The message in Figure 3-8, page 50 consists of a series of blanks, with a number under each. When the blanks are filled in as described below, a message will appear.

Read the description for each number, on page 51. (See Appendix 2 if you are uncertain about meanings of any terms used.) Find the polygon or circle described by that number in Figure 3-7. Write the *letter* you find in the appropriate polygon or circle above the number which provided the clue, in the message. For example: Statement 1 on page 51 says "the square". The square in Figure 3-7 contains the letter *T*. Therefore, write *T* above all 1's in the message.

Note: *Inscribed* means "drawn inside" *Circumscribed* means "drawn around".

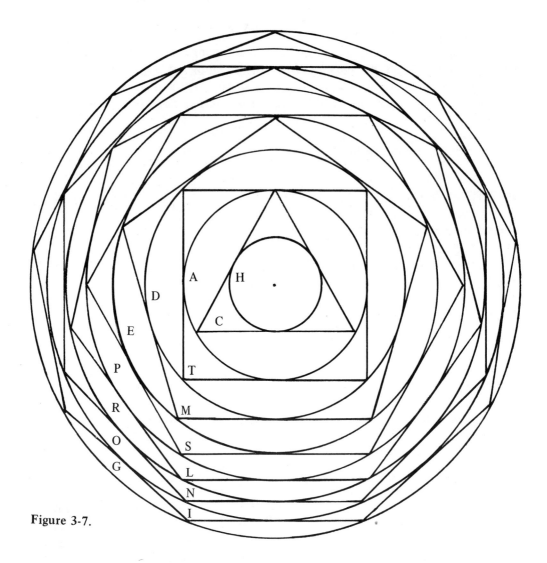

Figure 3-7.

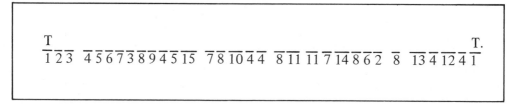

$$\frac{T}{1\ 2\ 3}\ \ \overline{4\ 5\ 6\ 7\ 3\ 8\ 9\ 4\ 5\ 15}\ \ \overline{7\ 8\ 10\ 4\ 4}\ \ \overline{8\ 11\ 11\ 7\ 14\ 8\ 6\ 2}\ \ \overline{8}\ \ \overline{13\ 4\ 12\ 4}\frac{T.}{1}$$

Figure 3-8.

1. The square
2. The circle inscribed in the triangle
3. The circle inscribed in the hexagon
4. The nonagon (The largest polygon in the diagram)
5. The octagon
6. The figure that circumscribes the smallest circle
7. The circle that circumscribes the heptagon
8. The circle that circumscribes the figure with the smallest number of edges
9. The hexagon
10. The circle that is inscribed in the pentagon
11. The circle that circumscribes the hexagon
12. The pentagon
13. The septagon
14. The circle that circumscribes the octagon
15. The circle that circumscribes the nonagon

Some Theory

The technique of *differentiation* divides smaller and smaller incremental changes in one variable by smaller and smaller changes in a related variable. These changes, observed over smaller and smaller intervals, form a series of ratios which approach a value called a *limit*. This limit is the end result of differentiation: the rate of change at the smallest interval—in effect, no interval at all—at the given instant or point.

   Integration may be interpreted as the limit of the *summation* of a *series* of elements—smaller and smaller segments of a curve, narrower and narrower rectangular regions under a curve, or flatter and flatter slices or cuboids in a three-dimensional figure. Integration can be thought of as a kind of addition. In fact, the symbol which represents integration, ∫, is the medieval symbol for "sum."

Maria Gaetana Agnesi   1718–1799

When the Marquise du Châtelet was 12 years old, Maria Gaetana Agnesi was born in Italy. Although born at a time and place when the best education for a woman was considered to be no education, Maria Gaetana Agnesi was to grow up to be an extraordinary woman, a mathematician of world renown.

Maria Agnesi would probably have seemed remarkable no matter when or where she lived. In the context of her own time and place, however, she stands out even more. In Italy during the eighteenth century, education for women was in a sorry state. Young women, even of the upper class, often could not read. It was a popular attitude of the day that women went astray from reading bad books—that it was quite enough for them to know how to recite the rosary. In Italy, as in France, girls of the upper class were customarily shut into convents as five-year-olds to await marriage. Education in these convents was rudimentary. Girls were taught little more than social accomplishments and dressmaking, perhaps with a bit of reading and writing thrown in. As adults, Italian women were expected to be decorous. It was not exactly frowned upon for them to be bright; it was merely considered unnecessary. All women were creatures of nature, and they were considered most attractive when they were unaffected and natural.

Some women did manage to become educated, however. If a girl was naturally gifted and her family did not prevent her, she might take advantage of tutors attached to the household as teachers for male children. Of course, this was only possible in upper-class families where tutors were employed.

Altogether Italy was a country of strangely contrasting attitudes toward women. Even though many upper-class women could neither read nor write, we hear of women who were lecturers and held university professorships. All in all, then, it was not extremely unusual that a girl such as Maria Agnesi, who was a prodigy, would have been encouraged by a father who was a mathematician.

Born in 1718, Maria Agnesi was to live a long time. Her career as a mathematician, however, was concentrated into only 20 of her eighty-odd years. This fact may be seen in her reply to a letter received when she was in her early forties. The letter was a request that she review an exciting new paper by the young French mathematician Laplace. In her reply she wrote that "such matters no longer occupy my mind."

The last 40 years of Maria's life were spent in service to the poor. Some sources say that Agnesi became a nun after her father's death. This seems to be a matter of some controversy. An early reference, an 1853 book by Sarah Josepha Hale called *Women's Record*, states that Maria Agnesi ". . . died in 1799, at Milan, where several years before she had taken the veil." Later references contradict this. In her sketch of Agnesi in *The Dictionary of Scientific Biography*, Edna Kramer writes that Agnesi expressed a strong desire to enter a convent, but was dissuaded by her father.[2] Kramer is in agreement with Sister Mary Thomas à Kempis, who wrote an article about Agnesi called "The Walking Polyglot." Sister Mary admits that the rumor that Agnesi became a nun ". . . even found its way into . . . encyclopedias, newspapers, and books of history." However, she adds, even *had* Agnesi joined the religious community after her father's death, she could not have died in it "as some of her biographies state, since the order which is mentioned was suppressed 17 years before her death."[3]

Whichever is the truth, everyone agrees that Agnesi lived the simple religious life of a nun, and she is venerated as though she had been one.

Young Woman

Like Hypatia's father, Pietro Agnesi was a mathematician. At the time Maria, the eldest of 21 children, was born, her father was already professor of mathematics at the University of Bologna. The Agnesi family was both cultured and wealthy.

That Maria was a gifted child was evident very early. By 9 or 11 or 13 (different sources give different ages) she spoke Greek, Hebrew, French, Spanish, and many other languages. Her grasp of Latin was outstanding. This was important since at the time Agnesi lived Latin was the language used by scholars all over Europe to enable them to communicate, despite the barriers of language.

As a young woman, Maria starred at gatherings in her home, where intellectuals from Italy and abroad would meet to hear her speak and to engage her in abstract mathematical and philosophical discussions. Maria would discourse on many topics in many languages. During intermissions Maria's younger sister, a gifted composer as well as an accomplished musician, would entertain on the harpsichord.

By the time she was 21, Maria begged to withdraw from these gatherings. She had always been shy, and had found them distasteful from the first. Her mother's death provided the excuse she needed. She took over management of the household, with its enormous number of children, and retired from public life.

The Productive Years

The education of her brothers had long been one of Maria's major preoccupations. Now as she was raising the large family, she concentrated in the next 20 years on her own development in mathematics. One of her famous books on analysis was said to have been written as a text for one of her brothers.

Maria Agnesi never married. We do not know why. Certainly her family did not lack the means to provide a suitable dowry. Perhaps she was not pushed toward marriage, since she was a good housekeeper, and housekeepers for families of 20 children were not much easier to find then than now. Probably she was not suited for marriage temperamentally. At a time when every well-born Italian woman wanted to have three men available to her (one for love [*il bello*], one for errands [*cicisbo* or *il brutto*], and one who paid the bills [*il buono*]) Maria Agnesi had no such wish. Modest and retiring, she took pleasure in living a life rich in the mind and rich in service to others.

Maria Agnesi started the work for which she became famous when she was about 20 years old. It occupied all her intellectual attention for about 10 years. Her level of concentration was said to have been extraordinarily intense, filling her sleeping hours as well as her waking ones. A story is told about the way she would sometimes solve a difficult problem. After struggling unsuccessfully with it, she would give up exhausted and go to bed. Once asleep, she would rise, still asleep, go to her study, write out the complete solution, and then return to bed. The next morning she would discover the problem at her desk, completely solved.

When her two-volume work *Analytical Institutions* was published, it created a great deal of excitement. Newton and Leibniz had recently invented the calculus. Materials on this subject were dispersed throughout many papers in many languages. Maria hoped to bring this material together in a clear way. She succeeded so well that her book became a model for clarity; it was widely translated and used as a textbook.

The publication and success of this work brought Maria Agnesi a triumph which was not merely personal. Hers was considered a triumph for women in general. She had demonstrated that women could indeed excel in the world of abstract reasoning: that there was no essential difference between the male and female intellect.

Maria's dedication for her masterpiece is interesting as a feminist statement. The book is dedicated "Her Sacred Imperial Majesty, Maria Teresa of Austria, Empress of Germany, Queen of Hungary, Bohemia, etc. etc.

> *. . . none has encouraged me so much as the consideration of your sex, to which Your Majesty is so great an ornament, and which, by good fortune, happens to be mine also. It is this consideration chiefly that has supported me in all my labours, and made me insensible to the dangers that attended so hardy an enterprise. For, if at any time there can be an excuse for the rashness of a Woman, who ventures to aspire to the sublimities of a science, which knows no bounds, not even those of infinity itself, it certainly should be at this glorious period, in which a Woman reigns, and reigns with universal applause and admiration. Indeed, I am fully convinced, that in this age, an age which, from your reign, will be distinguished to latest posterity, every Woman ought to exert herself, and endeavour to promote the glory of her sex, and to contribute her utmost to increase*

Maria Theresa (1717–1780). Maria Agnesi dedicated her major work, *Analytical Institutions*, to "Her Sacred Majesty, Maria Theresa of Austria, Empress of Germany, Queen of Hungary, Bohemia, etc. etc. ... none has encouraged me so much as the consideration of your sex, to which Your Majesty is so great an ornament, and which by good fortune, happens to be mine also. ...if at any time there can be an excuse for the rashness of a Woman, who ventures to aspire to the sublimities of a science, which knows no bounds, not even those of infinity itself, it certainly should be at this glorious period, in which a Woman reigns, and reigns with universal applause and admiration."

that lustre, which it happily receives from Your Majesty; who, having diffused, on all sides, the fame and admiration of your actions, have obliged Mankind to apply to you, with much greater reason, what has been said of some of the ancient Caesars; . . . that, by the justice and clemency of your Government, you are an honour to human nature, and a near resemblance of the divine.[4]

From Mathematics to the Poor

Uncertainty about the facts of Agnesi's life goes beyond whether or not she ever became a nun. There is also disagreement over whether or not she was actually a professor at the University of Bologna. Most writers agree that she was probably offered her father's chair on his death. Edna Kramer writes that in September 1750, Pope Benedict XIV, appointed her to the chair of mathematics and natural philosophy at Bologna. She adds, however, that "Agnesi, always retiring, never actually taught at the University of Bologna."[5] Instead, she accepted the position as an honorary one during the last two years of her father's life, and at his death withdrew from all scientific activity. John Colson however, in his introduction to the English translation of *Analytical Institutions*, refers to Agnesi, the very learned, ingenious, and celebrated Lady of Milan, as "a member of the University of Bologna, and lately advanced by the Pope to a Professorship in Mathematics and Philosophy in the same University."[6]

A clue to this confusion may perhaps be found in a statement by the editor of *Analytical Institutions*, who expressed the desire to include some biographical information about the author in the book: "but the confusion and misery which have been brought upon a great part of Europe, and particularly upon Italy, by the French Revolution have deprived me of the means of getting authentic information respecting this *Phenomenon* of Literature from the University of Bologna, of which she was once an ornament."[7]

Whatever the exact details, everyone agrees that by conscious choice Agnesi retired early, at the height of her powers, from mathematics and scholarship. Her deeply religious nature led her to spend the rest of her life in the service of the poor and sick. Ultimately she became the director of a hospital for the sick and indigent.

Maria Agnesi was to live to be an old woman. She died in 1799 when she was 81 years old. Her mathematical achievements are unquestioned. Had she not left mathematics at an early age, she might have ranked among the very greatest mathematicians.

In Maria Agnesi we see an example of the values that feminists hope will be the unique contribution of women to society. Free at last to develop their minds and take their places with men in the intellectual world, women will hopefully at the same time, retain their special feminine qualities of nurturing and caring. Perhaps they will be able to share these qualities with men as well.

Maria Gaetana Agnesi was born in the year __ __ __ __ .
The first two digits of the year are the seventh prime number.
The first and third digits are the same.
The fourth digit is 2^3.

Maria Agnesi lived to be 3^4 years old.

She died in __ __ __ __ .

Maria Gaetana Agnesi's Work

Analytical Institutions, Maria Agnesi's major work, was published in 1748 and brought her instant recognition in the academic circles of Europe. It represented 10 years of concentrated thought covering an enormous range of material. Its two volumes formed a complete and integrated treatment of algebra and analysis. In the second volume, on analysis, Agnesi used the new ideas and techniques of the calculus. Here mathematicians were trying to develop ways to deal with problems involving infinite quantities. Although a large part of the book organized material developed by others, Agnesi added many methods and generalizations of her own.

The Witch of Agnesi

Agnesi's name is most frequently used in connection with a curve having the amusing name "the Witch of Agnesi". Many people who have heard of the curve are not aware that Agnesi was a woman. Ironically, she was not the discoverer of this curve. The French mathematician Fermat is said to have written about it in 1665, almost a hundred years before. Even the word *witch* is the result of an inaccurate translation by an English admirer. However, since Agnesi did work with this curve in the analytic geometry section of her book, and since it is an interesting curve as well, we include the Witch of Agnesi as the activity here.

Three Ways to Generate the Curve . . .

The Witch of Agnesi starts with a circle and a line (Figure 4-1).

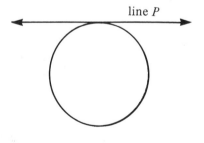

line *P*

Figure 4-1.

Figure 4-2 shows the circle and the line on coordinate axes X, Y. Line *P* is *tangent* to the circle at the *y*-axis, and therefore *parallel* to the *x*-axis.

Our plan is to find points *F* which are on the Witch of Agnesi. (Refer to Appendix 3 if you have forgotten how number pairs are represented as points in the plane.)

To find these points we do the following:

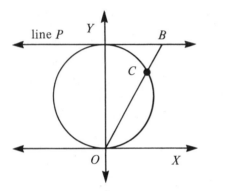

1. Choose any point *C* on the circumference of the circle.
2. Draw a line from *O* through *C*; it will intersect line *P* at some point *B* (See Figure 4-2). Remember that *O* is the origin—the intersection of the *x*-axis and the *y*-axis.

Figure 4-2.

3. Locate point *F* as the intersection of two lines: one through *B* and parallel to the *y*-axis; the other through *C* and parallel to the *x*-axis. The *x*-coordinate of *F* is the same as the *x*-coordinate of *B* and the *y*-coordinate of *F* is the same as the *y*-coordinate of *C* (See Figure 4-3).

4. Complete the left half of Table 4-1 by reading approximate values from Figure 4-5.

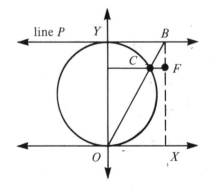

Figure 4-3.

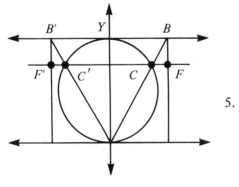

Figure 4-4.

5. Complete the right half of Table 4-1 by finding points *F'*. These points are reflections of points *F* through the *y*-axis. Their *x*-coordinates have the same numerical value but opposite sign. Their *y*-coordinates are the same.

Table 4-1.

C	Coordinates of points F		Coordinates of points F'	
	x (Read x-coordinate of B)	y (Read y-coordinate of c)	x' (read $-x$)	y' (same as y)
C_1	9	2	-9	2
C_2				
C_3				
C_4				
C_5				
C_6				
C_7				

6. Plot all points F and F' on Figure 4-5. Connect these points to see the Witch of Agnesi.

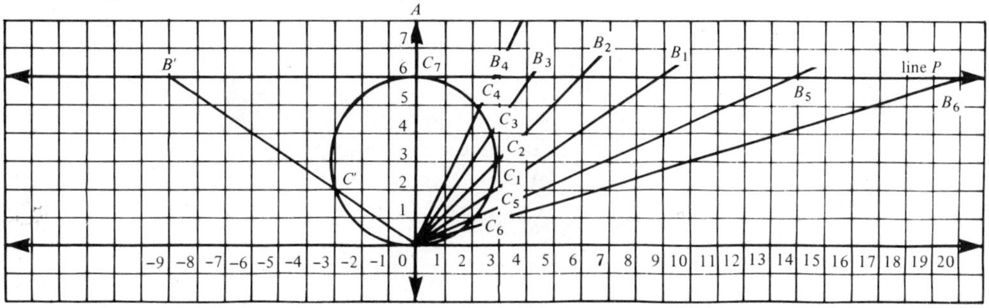

Figure 4-5.

Two other, less crude methods for generating this curve are developed in Appendix 4.

SOPHIE GERMAIN
PHILOSOPHE & MATHÉMATICIENNE
1776 — 1831

Sophie Germain 1776–1831

In 1776 the American Revolution began. At that same time in Paris a child was born who was to become an outstanding mathematician. Her name was Sophie Germain.

Although both Sophie Germain and Emilie du Châtelet were Frenchwomen, there were few similarities between their lives. In some important ways Sophie's life was more like that of du Châtelet's Italian contemporary Maria Agnesi. Both Sophie and Maria were daughters of wealthy, upper-class families. Both women lived austere personal lives; neither married nor had children. In their education these two women were very different, however. Agnesi's talents were recognized early by her mathematician father, who seemed to have no personal prejudices about the suitability of education for women. Maria, a gifted child, had been encouraged, tutored, and even pushed by her father from the very first.

Sophie Germain's parents were very different. They did not seem to share the attitude of the French upper classes, where sparkling intellectual conversation was valued and encouraged in women as well as men. Their attitude toward women seemed more English. They viewed "brain work" as a dangerous strain on the minds of young women.

Sophie Germain had a strong mind of her own, however, and her determination to educate herself was not to be denied. Fortunate in having access to her father's fine library, she managed to educate herself successfully with no outside help or tutoring of any kind.

The Struggle to Learn

Sophie Germain's parents were fairly wealthy. Her father referred to himself as a merchant; late in his life he became a director of the Bank of France.

A story, probably apochryphal, is told of the event that inspired Sophie's single-minded resolve to discover the excitement of mathematics. The French Revolution and the fall of the Bastille occurred in 1789. Paris was a chaotic and dangerous city for a 13-year-old girl to be living in. Sophie's family was secure enough to protect themselves adequately. However, Sophie was confined closely to home. The lonely girl must have found the richness and variety of her father's library a great help during those long quiet days. As she was reading one day she came upon the story of the death of the

Greek mathematician Archimedes. The story relates that during the invasion of his city by the Romans Archimedes was so engrossed in the study of a geometric figure in the sand that he failed to respond to the questioning of a Roman soldier. As a result he was speared to death. How fascinating the problem must have been to command such intense concentration! Sophie was certain that she wanted to learn all she possibly could about this fascinating subject which could inspire such attention—mathematics.

Her father's library was very good, but it did not contain all the materials she needed. Even worse, her parents were very difficult. They were worried about her; they felt that girls should not be straining their minds on such nonsense. Sophie might become ill. The exact nature of the danger was rather vague, but one thing was quite clear: the situation was dangerous.

Genuinely concerned, her parents did everything they could to discourage their daughter's studying. When they found her working late into the night, they took away her heat and light in order to force her to sleep. They hid her clothes. However, nothing they did seemed to stop her. After her parents were asleep she would light the candles she had hidden and work wrapped in quilts long into the morning in the freezing cold. One morning her parents found her asleep at her desk, the ink frozen, calculations covering her slate. It was finally obvious even to her parents that they would not be able to stop her. And so at last they allowed her to do what she was so determined to do. Still without a tutor, she spent the Reign of Terror—that unsettled time in France after the revolution—teaching herself differential calculus.

The Young Mathematician: The Struggle Continues

By the time Sophie was 18, France was settling back to normal, and the *Ecole Polytechnic* was founded. This was a technical academy established to train mathematicians and scientists for the country. Many of the outstanding French mathematicians of the time were lecturers there. This would have been an excellent place of study for the gifted young woman. But another obstacle appeared: women were not admitted to the academy as regular students.

Again, Sophie was not to be stopped by a mere regulation. From her friends she managed to obtain lecture notes for courses in which she was particularly interested. Lagrange's lectures on analysis seemed especially exciting. The ideas here were new and important.

At the end of each term, Polytechnic students customarily submitted reports. Under the pen name *M. LeBlanc,* Sophie Germain submitted a paper on analysis to Lagrange. He was so impressed by its originality that he wanted to meet the author in order to congratulate "him" personally on "his" paper. When he discovered that the author was a woman he was astounded. But Lagrange behaved in a way that is not atypical of truly great men.

Instruction in chemistry at the École Polytechnique, Paris. Note the absence of women in the lecture hall. Although women were not admitted to the recently organized École Polytechnique, the eighteen year old Sophie Germain was able to obtain the lecture notes of courses given there.

Although bound by the prejudices of their society concerning the abilities of women in general, they are supportive once confronted with the "exceptional" woman. Although the rules of society may deny even to these outstanding women formal admission to universities, membership in academies, and faculty chairs at universities, eminent men will often help women get at least some of what they need. How incredibly gifted a woman must have been, however, to survive and grow under such constraints. Only very few did; we will never know about those who did not.

Once Lagrange had discovered his "Monsieur LeBlanc" he became a great help and encouragement to her. He introduced Sophie to all the French scientists of the time. From then on, much of her education took the form of correspondence with other scholars. She continued to be self-conscious and shy about being a woman, however. In 1801, when she decided to write to the great German mathematician Gauss about some interesting results she had obtained in number theory, she worried that Gauss might not treat the correspondence seriously if he knew she was a woman. So she again became M. LeBlanc, Polytechnic student. Perhaps she need not have worried. Gauss, like Lagrange, continued to be very generous in praising her work even after he learned her true identity. This support was remarkable for any man of his generation; for a German, it was almost unprecedented.

In 1807 the French troops were occupying Hanover, where Gauss lived. Sophie, perhaps remembering the story of Archimedes, worried about Gauss's safety. The French commander of the occupation was a friend of the Germain family. Sophie contacted him and asked him to protect Gauss. It was as a result of this intervention that Gauss discovered that "Monsieur LeBlanc" was a woman. He paid her a high compliment in a letter.

> *But how describe to you my admiration and astonishment at seeing my esteemed correspondent Mr. Leblanc metamorphose himself into this illustrious personage [Sophie Germain] who gives such a brilliant example of what I would find it difficult to believe. A taste for the abstract sciences in general and above all the mysteries of numbers is excessively rare; one is not astonished at it; the enchanting charms of this sublime science reveal themselves only to those who have the courage to go deeply into it. But when a person of the sex which, according to our customs and prejudices, must encounter infinitely more difficulties than men to familiarize herself with these thorny researches, succeeds nevertheless in surmounting these obstacles and penetrating the most obscure parts of them, then without doubt she must have the noblest courage, quite extraordinary talents and a superior genius. Indeed nothing could prove to me in so flattering and less equivocal manner that the attractions of this science, which had enriched my life with so many joys, are not chimerical, as the predilection with which you have honored it.* [1]

The Mature Mathematician

Sophie Germain worked in number theory, and she won several prizes for her work in mathematical physics, particularly on problems of acoustics and elasticity. Some of the prizes she won in this field came as a result of an appeal by the French Academy for papers formulating a mathematical theory to explain and predict the unusual patterns that the German physicist Ernst Chladni was demonstrating in sand on vibrating plates. (Chladni's figures were fascinating to another woman mathematician, Mary Somerville, and we have included these diagrams as an activity in the chapter on her; see page 83.)

In 1816 Germain submitted her prize-winning paper. This paper, bearing her own name, won her the grand prize. It was the high point in her career. The paper stated a law for vibrating elastic surfaces which was described by a fourth-order partial differential equation, and which predicted what was happening in the Chladni figures.

Sophie Germain died in 1831 at the age of 55. She had been in great pain for two years, suffering from breast cancer. She died just a short time before she was to receive an honorary doctor's degree from the University of Göttingen. There she was also to have finally met Gauss, who had recommended that the honorary degree be granted to her.

Sophie Germain was one of the illustrious company of women who have been denied admission to the French Academy because they were women. She shares this distinction with Maria Agnesi, Sonya Kovalevskaya, and perhaps the most famous of all, the Nobel laureate in chemistry, Marie Curie.

Sophie Germain was born during the year of the American Declaration of Independence.

The last two digits of the year of her death are the eleventh prime number

Sophie Germain lived from __ __ __ __ to __ __ __ __ .

Sophie Germain's Work

Since Sophie Germain made important contributions to two very different branches of mathematics, we include activities in both. Her contribution to pure mathematics was in an area called number theory. Her later work was in applied mathematics; where she solved problems in acoustics and elasticity.

A Problem in Number Theory

Some of the most difficult problems in number theory, which continue to puzzle trained mathematicians, can be understood by people with little mathematical background. We shall try, step by step, to understand the statement of an important problem Sophie Germain solved in number theory. To try to understand her solution, however, would be far beyond the scope of this book.

In a letter to one of his friends, Gauss wrote about two theorems called the two test-theorems: "among the most beautiful things and the most difficult to prove." "Sophie Germain", he wrote, "has sent me the proofs of these; I have not yet been able to go through them, but I believe they are good."[2]

Two Statements

The first: $x^3 \equiv 2 \pmod{p}$ means x^3 leaves a remainder of 2 when divided by prime p.
The second: $x^4 \equiv 2 \pmod{p}$ means x^4 leaves a remainder of 2 when divided by prime p.

The problem is that sometimes these statements have solutions; sometimes they do not have solutions. Whether or not solutions exist depends on the particular prime (p) substituted in the statement. The "two test-theorems" tell the primes for which the statements will have solutions. Let's try to understand what this is all about.

Understand the Terms

Table 5-1.

	Column	1	2	3	4
	Row	x	$k_1 \bmod(3)$	$k_2 \bmod(5)$	$k_3 \bmod(7)$
$x \equiv k \bmod(p)$	1	5	2	0	5
	2	7	1	2	0
	3	8	2	3	1
	4	9	—	4	—
	5	10	1	—	—
	6	12	—	—	5
	7	15	—	—	—

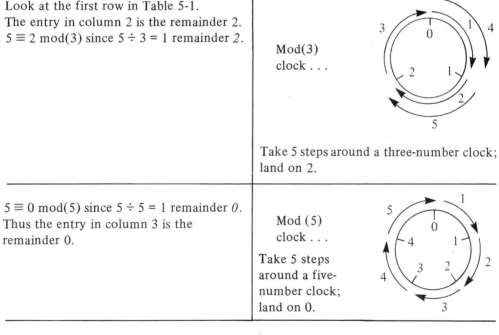

Look at the first row in Table 5-1.
The entry in column 2 is the remainder 2.
$5 \equiv 2 \bmod(3)$ since $5 \div 3 = 1$ remainder *2*.

Mod(3)
clock . . .

Take 5 steps around a three-number clock; land on 2.

$5 \equiv 0 \bmod(5)$ since $5 \div 5 = 1$ remainder *0*.
Thus the entry in column 3 is the
remainder 0.

Mod (5)
clock . . .

Take 5 steps
around a five-
number clock;
land on 0.

$5 \equiv 5 \bmod(7)$ since $5 \div 7 = 0$ remainder 5.
Thus the entry in column 4 is the
remainder 5.

Visualize this on a seven-number clock.

Look now at the entry in column 3, row 2 of Table 5-1.

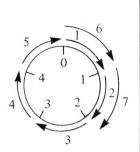

Seven steps around a five-step clock lands on 2. That is the same as saying

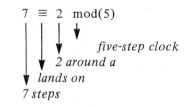

which is the same as saying

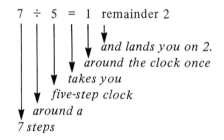

Looking now at column 3, row 4, in Table 5-1, we say 9 is congruent to ($\equiv$) 4 mod(5) since $9 \div 5 = 1$ remainder *4*. Remember, *congruence* ($\equiv$) defines a relationship between two numbers, in this case 9 and 4.

Complete Table 5-1 now. Notice that no value in any column will be greater than the modulus (mod) of that column. Why?

Now complete Table 5-2. Remember that $x^n = \underbrace{x \cdot x \cdot x \dots x}_{n \text{ times}}$; that is, $x^2 = x \cdot x$;

$x^3 = x \cdot x \cdot x$; $x^4 = x \cdot x \cdot x \cdot x$ and so on.

Table 5-2.

1	2	3	4	5	6	7	8	9	10	11	12	13	14
			$x^3 \bmod(p)$; p is a prime						$x^4 \bmod(p)$; p is a prime				
x	x^2	x^3	3	5	7	11	13	x^4	3	5	7	11	13
0	0	0						0					
1	1	1						1					
2	4	8	2					16					
3	9			2								4	
4							12	256					
5		125											
6						7						9	
7													
8		512						4096					
9				4						1			
10		1000								0			
11								14641				0	
12													
13		2197											0

Understanding the Question

Now we ask, which primes have solutions for $x^3 \equiv 2 \bmod(p)$ or $x^4 \equiv 2 \bmod(p)$? Look at the numbers in columns 4 through 8 and 10 through 14. Notice that 2 never appears in some of these columns. From the information in Table 5-2 complete Table 5-3 below.

Does 2 appear in the column? If it does, write *yes*, since a solution does exist. If not, write *no*, since a solution does not exist.

If your answer is *yes*, write the equation with the value of X that makes it true.

Table 5-3.

P	A solution exists for			
	$X^3 \equiv 2 \bmod(p)$		$X^4 \equiv 2 \bmod(p)$	
			Yes or No	Solution
3	yes	$2^3 = 8 \equiv 2 \bmod(3)$		
5	yes	$3^3 = 27 \equiv 2 \bmod(5)$		
7				
11				
13				

That is the problem. Try lots of cases. Look at what happens for different prime moduli. Do you see any pattern?

Vibration of Elastic Surfaces

In 1816 Sophie Germain won an important prize for her memoir on the vibrations of elastic plates. This prize, awarded by the French Academy of Sciences, was suggested by the work of Ernest Chladni. Chladni, a German physicist then living in Paris, had developed an interesting technique to study the vibration of elastic surfaces. After sprinkling fine powder on drumlike surfaces, he would set them vibrating by drawing a violin bow along their edge. These vibrations would cause patterns to appear in the powder. (See page 000 for more detailed description and pictures.) Chladni's results were attractive to look at, but what was even more important was that scientists knew no mathematics which would predict what was being seen. It was to encourage the solution to this problem that the French Academy offered its prize. Sophie Germain's success in winning the prize marked the high point of her career.

The mathematical technique used to solve this problem is known as the *calculus of variations*. Often the solution to a problem must satisfy a maximal or minimal condition. The calculus of variations finds such solutions mathematically. What does all this mean? Perhaps this story will help.

Maxima, Minima: an Example

Dido, Princess of an ancient city in Phoenicia, ran away from her home to settle on the northern coast of Africa. There she agreed to pay a specific price for as much land as could be enclosed by a bull's hide. Shrewdly, Dido cut the hide into very thin strips, tied the strips end to end, and proceeded to enclose an area having the total length of these strips as its perimeter. Choosing land along the sea so she need not enclose one edge, she decided that the length of the hide should form a semicircle. This curve was the correct solution to the problem of enclosing a maximum area with a fixed perimeter. The calculus of variations would find such a solution analytically.

Soap Films: A Two-Dimensional Model

Suppose a heavy snowfall has covered a town and some strenuous shoveling is needed to dig out. A solution to the following problem would probably be welcome.

What would be the shortest path which would connect your front door, mailbox, and garage? How about the front door, the mailbox, the garage, and the back door?

Soap films show nature's solutions to such minimal path problems. Because of surface tension, soap film is stable only if its area is a minimum. By experimenting with soap film, then, solutions can be found to problems which are extremely difficult to solve mathematically. Direct solutions would require the calculus of variations. Such solutions are often surprising.

How will it behave? Making a soap film demonstration model is not difficult if you have access to Plexiglas and the equipment to drill holes in it and cut it. Drilled holes represent points to be connected (See Figure 5-1). A nail, toothpick, or dowel is inserted through each hole, and then another sheet of plexiglass or glass is put on top to form a sandwich. Dip this sandwich into a soap solution. (One source says that liquid Woolite colored with vegetable dye works beautifully. Another recipe for the soap film is roughly equal amounts of water and commercial dishwashing detergent, with a small admixture of glycerin to stabilize the film.) The soap film path will appear in the sandwich.

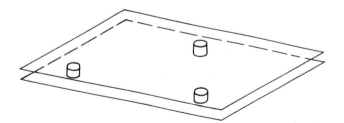

Figure 5-1.

Guess the shortest path which will connect these three points.

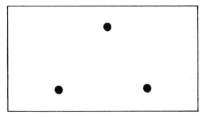

Can you guess the shortest path which will connect the four points in this figure?

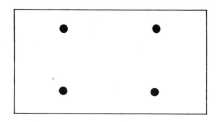

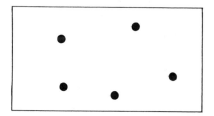

How about the following figure? Can you guess what the solution will look like here?

See page 80 for solutions.

The Common Property: A Construction. All these solutions have a common property: the paths all meet at 120° angles. You might try to show that these solution paths are indeed the *shortest* paths.

The proof that these minimal paths will meet at 120° angles is too complicated to do here. Instead, we include a related construction as the next activity. This activity locates a point *P* in a triangle such that lines from *P* to each vertex of the triangle will be the minimum path connecting the vertices.

Locate point P.
Lines connecting *P* to *A, B,* and *C* form 120° angles.

Find point *P* such that ∢ *APB* = ∢ *APC* = ∢ *BPC* = 120°.
(Note: this works only for triangles with no angle greater than or equal to 120°.)

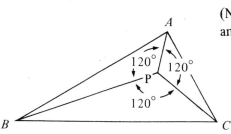

If you know enough geometry to try it anyway, see if you can discover on your own a compass-and-straightedge construction for locating this point.

If you cannot, then proceed with the construction as outlined below.

The basic concepts are simple. The constructions needed are not difficult. Here is a quick summary of what you will need to know how to do.

First construction: given a length, construct an equilateral triangle with the given length as one side.*

Concept: An equilateral triangle has three equal sides and three equal angles. The sum of the angles of any triangle is 180°. Therefore each of these three equal angles is 60°, since 180 ÷ 3 = 60°.

***Second construction:** bisect an angle.**

Concept: Remember, we are trying to *construct* a *120° angle*. If we first construct an isosceles triangle with two 30° angles, the third angle will be 120° since the sum of the angles of a triangle is 180°.

Third construction: Draw an arc of a circle spanning a 120° angle.

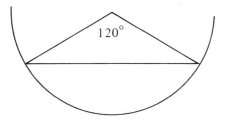

Concept: Such an arc is a set of points which share a common property: any point on that arc will be the vertex of a 120° angle when its rays cut the endpoints of the arc (where it intersects the circle). Here are two examples.

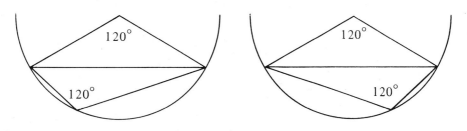

*See Appendix 5 if you've forgotten how to do this.

Now we're ready to begin.

1.   Given any triangle *ABC*, construct two equilateral triangles using each of two sides of *ABC* as edges. (For example, construct triangle *ACD* off *AC* and triangle *ABE* off *AB*.) Angles *DAC, DCA, ADC, EAB, BEA,* and *EBA* all equal 60°.

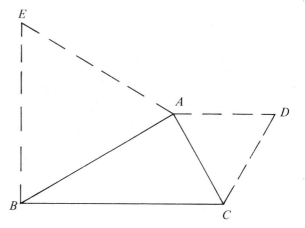

2.   Bisect ∢*CAD* and ∢*ACD*. Locate the intersection of these bisectors at *F*. Since ∢*FAC* and ∢*FCA* are each halves of 60° angles, they are each 30°. Therefore ∢*AFC* = 120° since the sum of all angles of a triangle equals 180°.

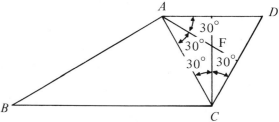

3. Using compass, construct the arc of a circle with center (pin) at *F* and with *AF* or *FC* as radii (width of compass). All points on arc *AC* will form 120° angles when connected to points *A* and *C*. For example, ∢*AGC* = 120° and ∢*AHC* = 120°.

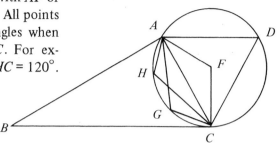

4. Repeat steps 2 and 3 for angles EBA and BAE.

5. Mark the intersection of the two arcs. Call the intersection *P*. Connect *P* to *A*, *B*, and *C*. Since *BPA* is 120° (it is on the arc whose points all form 120° angles with *A* and *C*) then *BPC* is also 120° (since sum of the angles around point *P* is 360°).

AP + *BP* + *PC* is the minimal path which connects points *A*, *B*, and *C*.

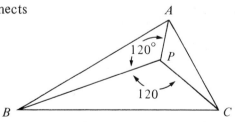

Locate (construct) points *P* on the following diagrams.

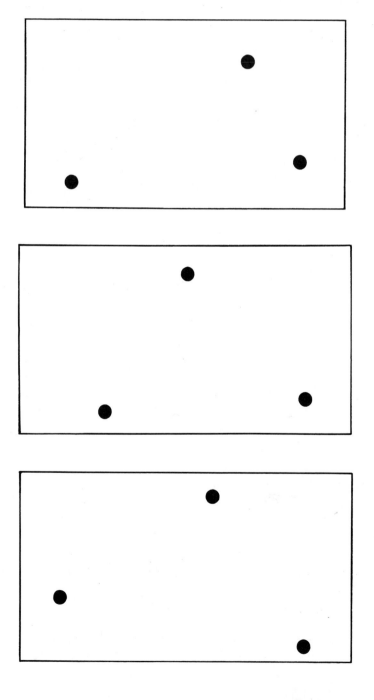

The soap bubble: a three-dimensional model.

Surprising solutions appear in the 3-dimensional equivalent of this problem. Again, soap film shows the result dramatically. These experiments are actually easier to do, since nothing so special as plastic drilling equipment is needed. All that is required here is some wire and the soap film or liquid plastic Dip-It.

Form wire into a polyhedron. Perhaps start with a tetrahedron or cube. Later go on to an octahedron. Do you remember the shapes of these figures? Look at the diagrams. Fill in Table 5-4.

Table 5-4.

Figure	Name	Number of faces	Number of edges	Number of vertices
	tetrahedron			
	cube			
	octahedron			

Faces: the planes which bound the solid. Faces are polygons.
Edges: the intersections of the planes or faces. Edges are lines.
Vertices: the intersections of the edges. Vertices are points.

Construct each wire figure with an extra edge for a handle. Then dip the figure, or look at the diagrams on p. 81. Describe the film surfaces formed on the tetrahedron:
How many film surfaces have been formed?
What are the shapes of the surfaces?
How many surface edges meet at each vertex?
Do these surfaces meet at 120° angles?
What do you guess the film formed on the cube will look like? Are you surprised by the solution?
How many surfaces do you see?
What are the shapes of the surfaces?
Remember, the total surface area of the film is the minimal surface that will connect the edges of the figure.
Try other shapes too: spirals, pretzels, coils, and so on.
You will probably be delightfully surprised by many of the results. Some fascinating articles and books have been written about soap bubbles (see bibliography). These are recommended reading if you find you are really interested.

Solutions to two-dimensional problem:

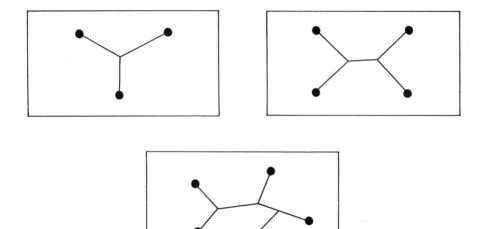

Two solutions to three-dimensional problems.

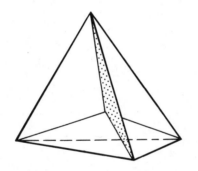

Mary Fairfax Somerville 1780–1872

Sophie Germain was four years old when Mary Fairfax Somerville was born in Scotland. The year was 1780. The American Revolution was nearly over. The Industrial Revolution had just recently begun, and with it came a new surge of interest in science and technology. Explorers were making discoveries in many fields. Everything was interesting to investigate—the shape of the earth, the seas and the rivers, biology, astronomy, and geology.

Mary Somerville's life was to be a long one. She lived to see and write about many of these new discoveries in science and mathematics. As a popularizer of science during a period when popular interest in science was great, her contribution was important.

Mary Somerville lived to be 92. She died peacefully in her sleep, a fortunate woman, having been granted one of her dearest desires: her mental faculties were unimpaired to the end.

Mary Somerville's story is similar in many ways to that of Sophie Germain. Both were self-educated women. Both struggled against the opposition of parents who thought the study of mathematics strange and dangerous for women. Although they were from different countries, the families of the two women shared the prevailing attitudes of their class toward education for women.

When Mary Somerville was growing up, education in England and Scotland was primarily a family responsibility. Schooling was not compulsory. For women, schooling was particularly sketchy and haphazard. Among the lower classes urban charity schools taught both girls and boys the rudiments of reading to make the Bible accessible to them. Daughters of the wealthy in England were not brought up and educated in convents, as was the custom on the continent. In England, the overthrow of the Roman Catholic Church had included the expropriation of church properties. Those facilities which had provided education for girls were not replaced. Many of these holdings were taken over by Oxford and Cambridge, universities for men.

Girls of the upper classes were taught the elements of reading and writing at home, often by their parents. In families that employed a tutor for male children, some of the tutor's attention might fall to the sisters of his pupils. But the competence of most gentlewomen was restricted to the reading of novels, the writing of letters, and the casting of household accounts. Later in the century the private boarding school, with its stress on deportment rather than on a solid education, catered to young ladies.

In some rare cases, girls, encouraged by book-loving fathers and having home libraries available, became scholars in their own right. But even these women were aware of the social constraints within which they must live their lives. One such woman, Lady Mary Wortley Montague, was a leading intellectual of the eighteenth century. As a grandmother, advising her daughter about the education of a precocious granddaughter, she urged the child be educated, yet added: "Conceal her learning . . . for the parade of it can only serve to draw on her the envy, and consequently the most inveterate hatred, of all he and she fools, which will certainly be at least three parts in four of all her acquaintance."[1]

Growing Up

Mary Somerville's life as a young girl was lonely but rich. The only daughter of a Scottish admiral, she grew up in Burtisland, a provincial village close to the sea. Her memoirs describe many hours spent exploring the seacoast. Her senses were keen, her eyes open to all she saw around her. Everything was interesting to her—the birds, the flowers, the stones, the water, the sky, the stars. "My mother taught me to read the Bible and to say my prayers morning and evening; otherwise she allowed me to grow up a wild creature."

Mary Somerville had a natural sensitivity to nature and its balance.

I never cared for dolls, and had no one to play with me. I amused myself in the garden, which was much frequented by birds. I knew most of them, their flight and their habits. . . . We fed the birds when the ground was covered with snow, and opened our windows at breakfast-time to let in the robins, who would hop on the table to pick up crumbs. The quantity of singing birds was very great, for the farmers and gardeners were less cruel and avaricious than they are now— though poorer. They allowed our pretty songsters to share in the bounties of providence. The shortsighted cruelty, which is too prevalent now, brings its own punishment, for, owing to the reckless destruction of birds, the equilibrium of nature is disturbed, insects increase to such an extent as materially to affect every description of crop. This summer (1872), when I was at Sorrento, even the olives, grapes, and oranges were seriously injured by the caterpillars—a disaster which I entirely attribute to the ruthless havoc made among every kind of bird.[2]

Mary was about nine years old when her father returned from a voyage to find that his "young savage" could read some but not yet write. She was promptly sent off to boarding school to correct the situation. From her accounts, she found this period distinctly unpleasant. At school Mary was perpetually in tears; the clothes worn by the girls were absurd. ". . . I was enclosed in stiff stays with a steel busk in front, while, above my frock, bands drew my shoulders back till the shoulderblades met. Then a steel rod, with a semi-circle which went under the chin, was clasped to the steel busk in my stays. In this constrained state I, and most of the younger girls, had to prepare our lessons."[3]

The "education" itself sounds equally absurd. "The chief thing I had to do was to learn by heart a page of Johnson's dictionary, not only to spell the words, give their parts of speech and meaning, but as an exercise of memory to remember their order of succession."[4] And then there was a lot of churchgoing. Since some of the girls were Presbyterians and some were members of the Church of England, the controversy over which church to attend was settled by going to both—kirk (Presbyterian) in the morning, church (Anglican) in the afternoon.

After a year Mary's formal education was essentially at an end. At home now, when the weather was bad, she found a few books she could read. "My mother did not prevent me from reading," she writes, "but my aunt Janet, who came to live in Burntisland after her father's death, greatly disapproved of my conduct. She was an old maid who could be very aggreeable and witty, but she had all the prejudices of the time with regard to women's duties, and said to my mother, 'I wonder you let Mary waste her time in reading, she never sews more than if she were a man.' Whereupon I was sent to the village school to learn plain needlework."[5]

When Mary was about 13 her mother took a small flat in Edinburgh for the winter; there Mary was sent briefly to writing school, where she learned to "write a good hand" and studied some simple arithmetic. At this time she also started to play the piano, which was to be a lifelong pastime.

Mary Somerville wrote of a wonderful summer visit to Jedburgh, home of the aunt and uncle who were later to become her in-laws.

For the first time in my life," she wrote, "I met in my uncle, Dr. Somerville, with a friend who approved of my thirst for knowledge. During long walks with him in the early mornings, he was so kind, that I had the courage to tell him that I had been trying to learn Latin, but I feared it was in vain; for my brother and other boys, superior to me in talent, and with every assistance, spent years in learning it. He assured me, on the contrary, that in ancient times many women—some of them of the highest rank in England—had been very elegant scholars, and that he would read Virgil with me if I would come to his study for an hour or two every morning before breakfast which I gladly did. I never was happier in my life than during the months I spent at Jedburgh.[6]

The Ladies' Diary (1704–1841): Cover, 1738. The Ladies' Diary, a contemporary magazine for women which contained many problems and puzzles in mathematics, was probably not the one referred to as having inspired Mary Somerville's interest in mathematics. (The Ladies' Diary contained no 'colored plates of dresses.') However, the problems included in it were probably of the same type.

The Discovery of Algebra

About this time Mary discovered the existence of a mysterious something called *algebra*. Shown a ladies' fashion magazine, which contained puzzles as well as colored plates of dresses, she discovered "what appeared to me to be simply an arithmetical question; but on turning the page I was surprised to see strange looking lines mixed with letters, chiefly *X*'s and *Y*'s, and asked; What is that? Oh, said Miss Ogilvie, it is a kind of arithmetic: they call it Algebra; but I can tell you nothing about it."[7]

It was not until much later that a tutor of her youngest brother helped her find out more. "He was a simple, good-natured kind of man, and I ventured to ask him about algebra and geometry, and begged him, the first time he went to Edinburgh, to buy me something elementary of these subjects."[8] Finally she had obtained what she so earnestly desired, and she set to work.

"Before I began to read algebra I found it necessary to study arithmetic again, having forgotten much of it. I never was expert at addition, for, in summing up a long column of pounds, shillings and pence, in the family account, it seldom came out twice the same way."[8]

The intensity of her study took her parents by surprise. Mary continued to spend her days doing the things young women usually did—mending, painting, playing the piano. Euclid was saved for nighttime. When the servants complained that the candle stock was being exhausted, her parents ordered her candle confiscated as soon as she was in bed. Her father expressed his concern to his wife; "Peg, we must put a stop to this, or we shall have Mary in a straitjacket one of these days."[9] This struggle is strongly reminiscent of that between Sophie Germain and her family.

As she grew older the pattern continued. During the days Mary practiced the piano (five hours a day), did housework, and gossiped with friends. She was fond of dancing, and often came home in broad daylight after dancing all night. She loved to paint and became an accomplished painter. She loved theater and concerts. She made all her own clothes, even her ball gowns. But through all this, she would rise at daybreak, dress, and—wrapped in a blanket against the cold—read algebra or the classics till breakfast time.

Marriage, Widowhood, and Remarriage

In 1804 Mary Somerville married Samuel Grieg, a captain in the Russian navy. He had a low opinion of the capabilities of all women and no interest in science. The couple lived in London, where Grieg had been appointed Russian consul. Mary's studies ended for the time being.

After only three years, her husband died. Twenty-seven years old now, widowed, and the mother of two young sons, Mary Somerville found herself financially independent for the first time in her life. For the first time she was free to manage her own life—free from control by parents or husband.

During this period Mary Somerville acquired the set of books, recommended by a professor friend, a mathematician at the University of Edinburgh, which was to be the closest she ever came to a formal professional education. Her excitement was high. "I could hardly believe that I possessed such a treasure when I looked back on the day that I first saw the mysterious word *Algebra*, and the long course of years in which I had persevered without hope."[10]

For the rest of her life, although she always enjoyed people, parties, and places, Mary Somerville devoted the first part of each day to her work. She would rise early and study or write for several hours. This done, she was available to friends or family or any amusements which might present themselves. With only brief interruptions, this became the major pattern of her life.

Her second marriage, in 1812, to her cousin William Somerville was the occasion of one of these interruptions. William Somerville was a surgeon in the British navy, a man of great intelligence but little personal ambition. Throughout their long, happy marriage he was extremely supportive of his wife's work, taking great pleasure in her success and fame.

Their daughter writes, "Rather than seek personal fame by writing about his own early travels in exotic lands . . . he was far happier in helping my mother in various ways, searching the libraries for the books she required, indefatigably copying and recopying her manuscripts, to save her time. No trouble seemed too great which he bestowed upon her; it was a labour of love."[11]

Not all the family was so uncritical of her work. While she and William were still engaged, Mary received a letter from one of her future sisters-in-law, who "hoped I would give up my foolish manner of life and studies, and make a respectable and useful wife to her brother."[12] Both Mary and William were outraged by this intrusion. They made their displeasure clear, and none of the family ever dared openly interfere again.

The Growth of Work and Fame

It was in 1827, when Mary Somerville was 47 years old, that she was launched on the project that was to establish her first fame. She was now the mother of two young daughters. A third, the eldest, had died in 1823, causing one of the great sorrows of Mary's life. Her daily routine now included supervision of the education of the two girls, Martha and Mary, as well as her own studies.

The important letter which began her public career came from Lord Brougham and was addressed to her husband. (This was a curiosity of the time. Even after she had become well known, much of Mary Somerville's correspondence with prominent colleagues was carried on through her husband.) In his letter, Lord Brougham proposed that Mrs. Somerville write a popularized account of Laplace's *Celestial Mechanics*. He hoped that this project would make this work available to a larger audience. A science writer was required: one who could communicate the concepts clearly without being too technical, without mathematical symbolism, and illustrated by facts and experiments that most people could understand. The ability to do this was to put Mary Somerville among the foremost ranks of scientific writers.

Uncertain of her ability, Mary undertook the work in secrecy. Should she fail, only those immediately involved need ever know. In her autobiography she writes of the tremendous pressures with which women, far more than men, must deal when they wish to be productive, without closing doors on society and friends.

> *I rose early and made such arrangements with regard to my children and family affairs that I had time to write afterwards; not, however, without many interruptions. A man can always command his time under the plea of business, a woman is not allowed any such excuse. At Chelsea I was always supposed to be at home, and as my friends and acquaintances came so far out of their way on purpose to see me, it would have been unkind and ungenerous not to receive them. Nevertheless, I was sometimes annoyed when in the midst of a difficult problem some one would enter and say, I have come to spend a few hours with you. However, I learnt by habit to leave a subject and resume it again at once, like putting a mark into a book I might be reading; this was the more necessary as there was no fireplace in my little room, and I had to write in the drawing-room in winter. Frequently I hid my papers as soon as the bell announced a visitor, lest anyone should discover my secret.*[13]

The job was finally done. The book, called *Mechanisms of the Heavens*, was a great success. It remained a popular text for higher mathematics and astronomy for years to come.

Support from her colleagues was generous and immediate. A letter from Dr. Whewell, later master of Trinity College, is dated November 1831. In it he writes, "I am glad that our young mathematicians in Trinity will have easy access to the book, which will be very good for them as soon as they can read it. When Mrs. Somerville shows herself in the field which we mathematicians have been labouring in all our lives, and puts us to shame, she ought not to be surprised if we move off to other ground, and betake ourselves to poetry . . ."[14]

Honors followed. In 1835 Mary Somerville and Caroline Herschel were elected the first women members of the Royal Astronomical Society. A pension of 200 pounds per year from the King of England came at a fortuitious time; the remainder of the Somervilles' inheritance had just been squandered by an adviser friend. When their financial misfortune became known, the pension was increased another 100 pounds.

As the years went on Mary Somerville continued to study and write. Each of her new publications was essentially a popularization and compilation of the contemporary state of knowledge in a scientific field. Her books sold well. Her second book, *Connection of the Physical Sciences*, was followed in 1848 by *Physical Geography*. Her last major work, in yet another field, was published when she was 89 years old: *Molecular and Microscopic Science* was a summary of the most recent discoveries in chemistry and physics.

Mary Somerville's autobiography contains notes of support from many friends and colleagues. Many of these are from women. A very old friend, Joanna Baillie, wrote with special pride of Mary's achievements. She wrote in 1832, "...I feel myself greatly honoured by receiving such a mark of regard [a copy of Somerville's book] from one who has done more to remove the light estimation in which the capacity of women is too often held, than all that has been accomplished by the whole sisterhood of poetical damsels and novel-writing authors."[15]

One of the most exciting letters of congratulation was from her old friend and colleague, Sir John Herschel. This letter was written, (still to *Mr.* Somerville) from the Cape of Good Hope, where Herschel was engaged in astronomical observations. He wrote of the King's pension as formal recognition of Mrs. Somerville's work:

> *Although the Royal notice is not quite so swift as the lightning in the selection of its objects, it agrees with it in this, that it is attracted by the loftiest; and though what she has performed may seem so natural and easy to herself, that she may blush to find it fame; all the rest of the world will agree with me in rejoicing that merit of that kind is felt and recognized at length in the high places of the earth. . . . I had almost forgotten that by a recent vote of the Astronomical Society I can now claim Mrs. Somerville as a* colleague. *Pray make my compliments to her in that capacity, and tell her that I hope to meet her there at some future session.*[16]

Ten years later Herschel addressed an interesting letter to Mrs. Somerville, this time directly. New observations by an Italian astronomer had come to his attention and he wished to have them confirmed. De Vico's accounts of the extremely powerful new telescope he is using sounded exciting, but Herschel didn't quite trust his colleague's enthusiasm. What are "the *real* powers and merits of De Vico's great refractor at the *Collegio Romano*?" he wrote.[17] Since Mary and Dr. Somerville were living in Italy at that time, Mrs. Somerville would be the natural person to make such a judgment—but this was impossible since the Collegio Romano was a monastery. "I fear me that these wonders are not for *female eyes*," Herschel wrote later; "the good monks are too well aware of the penetrating qualities of such optics to allow them entry within the seven-fold walls of their Collegio."[18] And so again we see an absurd situation: one of the scientists most qualified to make a judgment is prevented from doing so because she is a woman.

All her life Mary Somerville was sensitive to the restrictions placed on women both by society and by the inequities of British law. Even more absurd was the situation in the United States. She wrote that as a young woman she "took the anti-slavery cause so warmly to heart that I would not take sugar in my tea, or indeed taste anything with sugar in it."[19] And later in her life, the American law was even more insulting to women, granting suffrage to the newly emancipated slaves but still refusing it "to the most highly educated women of the Republic."[20]

Mary wrote passionately of the limitations on education for women in Great Britain. "Age has not abated my zeal for the emancipation of my sex from the unreasonable prejudice too prevalent in Great Britain against a literary and scientific education for women."[21]

Looking back during her later years, she considered that significant progress had been made in her own lifetime. "She took the liveliest interest in all that has been done of late years to extend high class education to women, both classical and scientific, and hailed the establishment of the Ladies' College at Girton as a great step in the true direction, and one which could not fail to obtain most important results. Her scientific library, as already stated, has been presented to this College as the best fulfilment of her wishes."[22]

Still, with all her understanding of the limitations which society placed on women, Mary Somerville herself seemed bound by the stereotypes of her time. Some of her writings indicate that she fundamentally doubted whether women were capable of *real* genius. She was not surprised to hear that a male colleague had extended some work she had written in a way she had not thought of herself. In an early draft of her autobiography she wrote, "If I had possessed originality or genius I might have done it. . . .I have perseverence and intelligence but no genius, that spark from heaven is not granted to the sex, we are of the earth, earthy, whether higher powers may be allotted to us in another existence God knows, original genius in science at least is hopeless in this."

The Last Years

Mary Somerville lived to be a very old woman. First with her husband and two daughters, who never married, and then with the daughters alone, she lived for many years in Italy, dying in Naples in 1872. Those who live to be very old must deal again and again with the loss of those to whom they are close. Mary Somerville faced such losses many times. In 1860 her husband died. In 1865 her son Woronzow Greig died. On the death in 1871 of Sir John Herschel, who was 10 years younger than she, she mourned another close and valued friend. "Few of my early friends now remain—I am nearly left alone."[23]

When she was 89 she wrote very beautifully about her feelings of immortality—for herself and for human beings in general—and touchingly about her tender feeling toward animals.

> *The short time I have to live naturally occupies my thoughts. In the blessed hope of meeting again with my beloved children, and those who were and are dear to me on earth, I think of death with composure and perfect confidence in the mercy of God. Yet to me, who am afraid to sleep alone on a stormy night, or even to sleep comfortably any night unless someone is near, it is a fearful thought, that my spirit must enter the new state of existence quite alone. We are told of the infinite glories of that state, and I believe in them, though it is incomprehensible to us; but as I do comprehend, in some degree at least, the exquisite loveliness of the visible world, I confess I shall be sorry to leave it. I shall regret the sky, the sea, with all the changes of their beautiful colouring; the earth, with its verdure and flowers: but far more shall I grieve to leave animals who have followed our steps affectionately for years, without knowing for certainty their ultimate fate, though I firmly believe that the living principle is never extinguished.*[24]

Mary Somerville died peacefully in her sleep. Shortly before her death she had written "I am now in my ninety second year (1872), still able to drive out for several hours; I am extremely deaf, and my memory of ordinary events, and especially of the names of people, is failing, but not for mathematical and scientific subjects. I am still able to read books on the higher algebra for four or five hours in the morning, and even to solve the problems. Sometimes I find them difficult, but my old obstinacy remains, for if I do not succeed today, I attack them again on the morrow. I also enjoy reading about all the new discoveries and theories in the scientific world, and on all branches of science."[25]

Mary Somerville was fortunate in realizing one of her greatest desires—to enjoy the full power of her mind as long as she lived.

The first two digits of the year of Mary Somerville's birth are the seventh prime number.

The last two digits form a number which is 10 times the sum of the first two digits.

The second and third digits of her birth and death years are the same, but reversed.

The last two digits of the year of her death are the number which is the product of the sum of the first two digits by the second digit.

Mary Somerville lived a long time, from __ __ __ __ to __ __ __ __ .

Mary Fairfax Somerville's Work

Mary Somerville wrote four immensely popular and influential books. These books, and the part they played in educating people about the new discoveries in science, were her major contributions. Each was an impressive treatment of what was known at the time in a given area of science.

Her first book was commissioned by the head of an organization called the Society for the Diffusion of Useful Knowledge. Lord Brougham, then High Chancellor of Britain, asked her to write the *Mechanism of the Heavens* in order to popularize an important new work in physical astronomy by the French mathematician Laplace. Somerville defined physical astronomy as "the science which compares and identifies the laws of motion observed on earth with the motions that take place in the heavens. . . ."[26] The book developed the concept that a wide variety of physical phenomena may be explained by the same few laws, as Newton had shown in his work.

The Pendulum and the Earth

In an early section on variable motion, Mary Somerville described the way in which scientists were able to draw conclusions about the shape of the earth by observing the motion of a simple pendulum. This seems an incredible leap, but with the help of a little mathematics it makes sense.

The equation which describes the motion of a simple pendulum is $T = \pi\sqrt{r/g}$, where r is the length of the pendulum, g is the gravitational field, and T is the time required for a pendulum to move through one swing (oscillation).

The time required to move through one swing does not depend on the distance through which the pendulum swings, since this distance is not a part of the equation. Time depends only on the length of the thread (r) and the intensity of gravitation (g).

The reasoning, then, from the pendulum to shape of the earth goes as follows: If the earth were a perfect sphere, g would be constant. "The intensity of gravitation would be the same in every point of its surface; because every point on its surface would then be equally distant from its centre."[27] Pendulum experiments show that g is not constant since it is necessary to increase the length of the string (r) to maintain constant periods (T) as one moves toward the poles. "The intensity of gravitation increases from the equator to the poles."[28] This shows that the earth must be flattened toward the poles. Explorer-scientists verified these theories experimentally.

From Pendulum to Cycloid

Mary Somerville described in detail the curve which models the motion of the pendulum. In her description, the pendulum is an oscillating particle. "It is now proposed to investigate the nature of the curve in which a particle must move, so as to oscillate in equal times, whatever the amplitude of the arcs may be."[29] The curve which has this property is the *cycloid*.

In his book *Mathematical Circles*, Howard Eves writes about the cycloid. "From the moment of its invention, the cycloid generated controversy."[30] Some called it the Helen of Geometry because of its beautiful properties. Some called it the Apple of Discord because of the quarrels it seemed to generate among mathematicians as they fought over credit for discovering its many properties. Since this curve shed light on several surprisingly different physical problems, there were many credits and many controversies.

The *cycloid* is a path of points, generated by a rolling circle. More specifically, it is a path generated by a point on the circumference of a circle as the circle rolls along a straight line.

To approximate a cycloid, construct a circle on a card, using a compass with radius 3.2 cm, or just trace and cut out the circle shown in Figure 6-1. Mark the rim (circumference) of the circle as shown, 0 through 19. Each section marked along the rim is approximately 1 cm long. Place a centimeter ruler (or the edge of this page) along a sheet of paper. Set 0 on circle to 0 on straight edge. (Use ruler or the marked edge on this page, Figure 6-2.) Roll this circle along the ruler, so that 1 on the rolling circle touches 1 on the ruler, 2 on the circle touches 2 on the ruler, etc. As each of these points coincide, mark the position on the paper of point 0. Join these points to form a path. This path of points will approximate a cycloid.

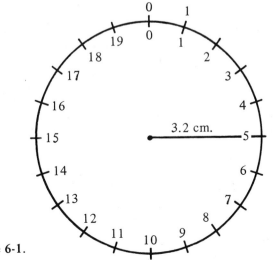

Figure 6-1.

Figure 6-2.

You may get the same effect by taping a piece of chalk to the inside of a coffee can (see Figure 6-3) and rolling the can along the ledge of a blackboard. The trace of the chalk on the blackboard will be a cycloid.

Figure 6-3.

The length of one arch described by the cycloid is four times the diameter of the circle which generated it. Do you see why? What is the length of this arc, generated by the circle with radius 3.2 cm? The area under one cycloid arc has been shown to be three times the area of the generating circle. What is the area of the figure you have generated?

If it is inconvenient to try the experiment described above, look at Figure 6-4, which is a time-sequence sketch of the cycloid. Compare this curve with the Witch of Agnesi. How many similarities do you notice? How many differences do you see?

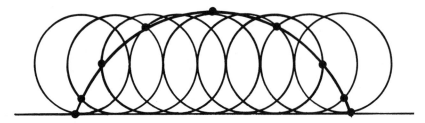

Figure 6-4. A curve traced by a point of a circle that rolls on the outside of a fixed circle is called an epicycloid.

Other Roulettes

Epicycloids

You can generate an epicycloid in the following way: Using two coins of equal value, roll one along the rim of the other. Trace the path of a point on the circumference of the rolling coin. What does the figure look like?

Try this for a rolling circle whose diameter is one-half the diameter of the path circle. What does the figure traced by a point on the rolling circle look like now? How about a figure made by two circles in the relation of 1:3? 1:4?

Hypocycloids

Suppose the rolling circle moves along the *inside* of a reference circle. The figures generated in this way are called hypocycloids.

To generate a hypocycloid, roll a jar lid or circle inside the rim of a pie plate. Fix a point on the rolling circle and mark the path of that fixed point along the plate. Here again, the relationship between the diameters of the rolling circle and the path circle will determine the shape of the curve described by the moving point. If the diameter of the rolling circle is one-third that of the path circle, the hypocycloid will look like the one in Figure 6-5. Can you predict the shape of the path when the rolling circle's diameter is half the diameter of the path circle? How about the shape of the figure when the ratio of the diameters is 1:4?

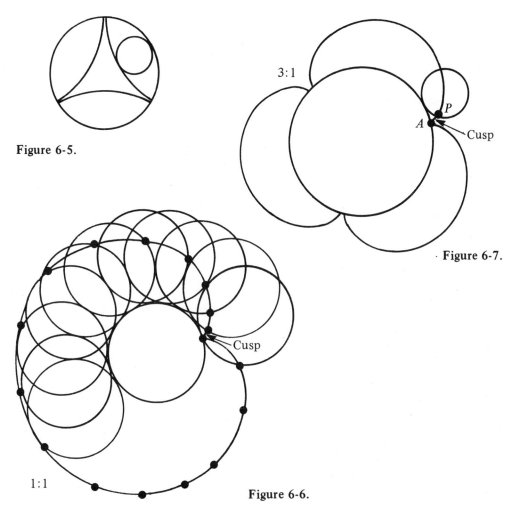

Figure 6-5.

3:1

P

A

Cusp

· Figure 6-7.

Cusp

1:1

Figure 6-6.

A Rolling Puzzle

Place any two coins of the same denomination in the relation shown in Figure 6-8. Roll the top coin around the rim of the bottom one. When the top coin is directly below the bottom one, will the faces of the two coins look like Figure 6-8 or Figure 6-9? Why do you think this is the case?

Figure 6-8.   Figure 6-9.

Chladni Diagrams

In *Connection of the Physical Sciences* (1854) Mary Somerville included a section on vibrations of surfaces, an area in which Sophie Germain did her prize-winning work. Here Somerville described Chladni's experiments and included diagrams of his results. Ernst Chladni was the German physicist who did fascinating experimental work on the vibrations of surfaces (see page 67). By spreading fine powder over glass plates, and running a violin bow over their edges, Chladni was able to observe the patterns of vibrations on the plates. Clearly visible lines (nodes) appeared as the powder collected at points of no motion. The most striking feature of all these nodal patterns was their bilateral (or reflection) symmetry. Figure 6-10 reproduces some of the plates in Mary Somerville's book. The opposite sides of the nodal lines represent opposing motions under vibration. "To Chladni is due the whole discovery of the symmetrical forms of the nodal lines in vibrating plates."[31]

The Symmetries of Nodal Lines

Use two colors to color each of these diagrams such that no adjacent edges are the same color. Because of the symmetries of the diagrams, only two colors are sufficient to do this. Notice that some of the diagrams, when colored, have reflection symmetry with respect to color as well as shape. Some diagrams have only symmetry with respect to shape. Which figures have both symmetries?

Figure 6-10. Diagrams of Chladni vibration plates from *Connection of the Physical Sciences.*

Ada Byron Lovelace 1815–1852

As a young woman, Ada Byron lived a life typical in many ways of young women of her class. The winter season was to be spent in London, the time there filled with concerts, theater, and parties—seeing and being seen in all the right places. If all went according to plan, an eligible man would presently appear and a suitable marriage would result.

Ada was involved in these social games, and yet her interests were much broader. Although it was usual for a young woman of her class to be educated, the education was typically superficial. Ada Byron was particularly lucky here. Several people close to her recognized and encouraged her mathematical talents when they appeared. Her mother had always enjoyed mathematics. Mary Somerville, who was then already quite famous, was a close friend of the family. Other friends of her mother's were Sophia and Augustus DeMorgan, the latter a well-known mathematician who eventually became Ada's tutor.

In this light, stories of Ada Byron's first interaction with Charles Babbage and his Difference Engine are not surprising. A visit to Charles Babbage's studio was considered a London sight not to be missed, and Ada Byron was taken there by Mary Somerville during Ada's second London season. The young woman's reaction on seeing this early computer is said to have made a significant impression on Charles Babbage, a widely-known inventor and scientist. When his computer was completed, Babbage claimed, it would be capable of calculating at speeds and accuracy far beyond the ability of any human being.

Sophia DeMorgan described the scene of the meeting. "While the rest of the party gaped at this beautiful instrument with the same sort of expression and feeling that savages are said to have shown on first seeing the looking glass, Miss Byron, young as she was, understood its workings and saw the great beauty of the invention."[1]

When he met Ada, Babbage already knew a little about this 18-year-old girl of unorthodox tastes. He knew she was Lord Byron's daughter. He also knew that Lord Byron was one of England's most famous poets, one whose life had been surrounded by scandal. What Babbage could not then know was how Ada Byron's life and work were to converge with his own. By the mid-twentieth century Charles Babbage would finally be recognized as a father of modern computers—and Ada Byron Lovelace as the first person to detail the process now known as computer programming.

Ada and Lord Byron

Augusta Ada Byron was born on December 10, 1815, in a house overlooking London's Green Park. Her mother, Annabella Milbanke, had been married to Lord Byron for little more than a year when their daughter was born. From the start the marriage had been strained and stormy. Byron was fiercely temperamental, passionate, perhaps even slightly mad. Annabella was very different: a cool rationalist with a strong interest in mathematics. Yet in spite of Byron's obvious pleasure in tormenting her, she adored her Bohemian poet. Raised largely in the country by devoted parents who had been married for 15 years before she was born, Lady Byron must have found her young husband's behavior toward her particularly painful and difficult to understand. A few months after Ada's birth, a curt note from her husband informed Lady Byron that she was to go home to her parents and await further word. "The child will, of course accompany you," he wrote. Marriage had become unbearable to him. He could hardly bring himself to acknowledge his daughter's birth, and was never to see her again.

Lady Byron adored their child and devoted the rest of her life to raising her alone. Hurt and sad at her husband's lack of interest in the girl, she was even more fearful that any interest he did have might lead to a demand for custody of the child. In England this was then the prerogative of the natural father, even for children born out of wedlock. And, from time to time, Byron did in fact threaten to take Ada from her mother to be raised by his sister Augusta—but he never actually did so.

Lord Byron died in Greece in 1824 when Ada was eight years old. On his deathbed, he wrote to his sister Augusta for news of his daughter. Lady Byron's reply tells us something of Ada Byron as a child. She wrote: "Her prevailing characteristic is cheerfulness and good temper. Observation. Not devoid of imagination, but is chiefly exercised in connection with her mechanical ingenuity . . . the manufacture of ships and boats etc. Prefers prose to verse, because puzzled by poetical diction. Not very persevering. Draws well. Open and ingenuous. Temper now under control. Tall and robust."[2]

The similarities and contrasts between Lord Byron and the daughter he barely knew are fascinating. Physically, the two are said to have been very much alike: Ada inherited her father's fine features and dark, romantic good looks. Both died young, at exactly the same age—36. In their lives, both experienced periods of great achievement and accomplishment as well as periods of scandal and disgrace. Yet for all their similarities, their interests and occupations were in stark contrast. George Byron was a poet and a political visionary; Ada Byron was a mathematician as well as an accomplished violinist and linguist.

Growing Up

Not much has been written about Ada's youth. We can be reasonably certain that her mathematical aptitude was recognized and encouraged by her mother, who had herself more than an average interest in mathematics. Byron had once referred to his wife as the Princess of Parallelograms.

In Mary Somerville's autobiography we come upon another influence on the young woman's development. "All the time we lived at Chelsea we had constant intercourse with Lady Noel Byron and Ada, who lived at Esher, and when I came abroad I kept up a correspondence with both as long as they lived. Ada was much attached to me, and often came to stay with me. It was by my advice that she studied mathematics. She always wrote to me for an explanation when she met with any difficulty. Among my papers I lately found many of her notes, asking mathematical questions. Ada Byron married Lord King, afterwards created Earl of Lovelace, a college companion and friend of my son."[3]

"Accomplished mathematician" was in no way a customary role for either women *or* peeresses, and Lady Lovelace, although she enjoyed more encouragement than many women, found that her special position created special problems. However, she was determined to study mathematics. Her search for a suitable tutor continued over many years. A letter written to Charles Babbage before she managed to persuade him to take on the tutorial role asks that he recommend someone for the job, but warns him to keep her name confidential while doing so. Engaging a tutor seems to have been considered unsuitable behavior for a noblewoman.

Marriage and Life as a Member of the Country Nobility

Ada Byron was married at nineteen to William, Lord King, who soon became the Earl of Lovelace. He was 10 years her senior yet was to outlive her by 40 years. All her references to him in her letters indicate that they enjoyed a warm relationship. His interest in and support of her work is always evident and often touching. In a letter to Babbage, Ada mentions that her husband is occupied just then "inking over" a paper which she had written in pencil.[4] (Typewriters had not yet been invented and copying had to be done by hand.) Intellectually, Ada Lovelace seems to have been her husband's superior, but this created no problems between them. Lord Lovelace accepted his wife's talents and seemed to take pride in her accomplishments.

The couple settled into the life of the country gentry and divided their time among three households—two in the country and the third in London. They had two sons and a daughter. The daughter's life was particularly interesting. After demonstrating an early gift for mathematics reminiscent of her mother and grandmother, Lady Anne Blount became a famous Arabic scholar.

Ada's relationship with her children was marked by absent-minded fondness. The details of raising them were left to others—to her husband, her mother, and servants. This, however, was not unusual among the English upper classes, and the children later recalled their mother with great affection.

Growth as a Mathematician

In a sense Ada Lovelace's work was also one of her children; it was of equal importance to her. In one letter to Babbage she seemed so pleased with a manuscript that she referred to it not only as a child but, significantly, as a *male* child. She wrote, "I am very much satisfied with this first child of mine. He is an uncommonly fine baby, and will grow to be a man of the first magnitude and power."[5]

Although Ada Lovelace showed great promise, her work never developed as far as it might have at another time. Conditions and attitudes common then must have been smothering to the scientific and mathematical talents of any young women. An extraordinary letter written by the mathematician Augustus DeMorgan, a family friend and for several years Ada's tutor, dramatizes this. The letter was written to Ada's mother, Lady Byron, when Ada was a grown woman of 28, married and herself a mother. In it DeMorgan warned Lady Byron of the dangers to her daughter's health in pursuing her talents and fully exercising her extraordinary gifts. From the quality and intensity of her powers, DeMorgan considered Ada capable of going far—much further, he suggested, than Mary Somerville, who at this time was quite famous. He doubted, however, that Ada's frail woman's body would be able to stand such strain.

Fearing that it might encourage her to "engage in such intense intellectual activity as to impair her health," DeMorgan never expressed his opinion to Lady Lovelace herself. "I have therefore," he wrote, "contented myself with very good, quite right and so on." He concludes his letter to Lady Byron with the request that it be kept confidential.[6]

Relationship with Babbage

Like her father, Ada was a gifted letter writer. Thanks to this, we have a detailed record of her relationship with Charles Babbage. Their letters, covering their 18-year relationship, are most interesting and revealing, often playful and even flirtatious. During this period Babbage was occupied with problems in the design and construction first of the Difference Engine, and later of the Analytical Engine—both precursors of our modern computers. Over the years, Ada's letters show an evolution from deferential student to self-confident coworker. As her own mathematical talents developed she was able finally to set down the first clear exposition of how to communicate with such machines, and, in effect, to present the first examples of how a computer may be programmed.

The first letter from Ada Lovelace to Charles Babbage is dated January 18, 1836. She was 21 years old and had been married one year. Very much the student, she sounded eager, polite, formal, and somewhat unsure of herself in her early letters. She told him of her eagerness to continue her mathematical education and that she was looking for a teacher.

Portion of Charles Babbage's Difference Engine. Upon seeing the machine during an early visit to Babbage's studio, Ada Byron, young as she was, 'understood its working and saw the great beauty of the invention.'[1]

She later wrote, "Do not reckon me conceited, for I am sure I am the very last person to think over highly of myself; but I believe I have the power of going just as far as I like in such pursuits, and while there is so very decided a taste, I should almost say a passion, as I have for them, I question if there is not always some portion of natural genius even. At any rate the taste is such that it *must* be gratified."[7]

By January 1841 she had developed an easier, more informal style. She wrote: "My dear Mr. Babbage. If you come by the rail-way on Friday, we will send the carriage to meet you . . . . Bring warm coats or cloaks as the carriage will probably be an open one. If you are a skater, bring skates to Ockham; that being the fashionable occupation here now, and one I have much taken to."[8]

At this time Ada was beginning to formulate her "grand plan". Tentatively, in the same letter she wrote: "It strikes me that at some future time (it might be even within three or four years, or it might be many years hence) my head may be made by you subservient to some of your purposes and plans. If so, if even I could be worthy or capable of being used by you, my head will be yours."[9]

The Project

Her chance came sooner than Ada had imagined. In October of the following year (1842) L. F. Menebrea, an Italian mathematician and ambassador to France, delivered a paper at a meeting in Geneva describing the function and theory of Babbage's Analytical Engine. Ada proposed that she translate the paper from the French in order to make it available to English readers.

Much of the correspondence between her and Babbage deals with the period during which this work was going on. By July 1843 she seemed happy with her progress on the work and described her own writing style as amazing her with its "pithy and vigorous nature." "I am quite thunderstruck," she continued, "at the power of the writing. It is especially unlike a woman's style surely; but neither can I compare it with any man's exactly."[10]

As the project developed it became much more extensive than had originally been intended. It became an annotated translation accompanied by a set of notes which elaborated the original, making it three times as long. The new work was so superior to the original that Babbage thought it should be an original paper. Lady Lovelace disagreed, feeling that she had made a commitment to the publishers to produce the translation and could not renege on this original agreement.

In the final weeks of the preparation of the manuscript, letters flew back and forth between them, often hand-delivered by servants who stand by as replies were written. Ada's confidence had grown considerably, and she now signed her letters in such teasing and affectionate ways as "Yours Puzzlepate" or "Addlepate" when confused or harassed.

Toward the end she began to lose patience with Babbage's rather careless work habits. He lost material! He forgot to note corrections! He made revisions without her permission and in so doing confused her meaning! In an exasperated letter dated July 28, 1843, she wrote: "The missing part must be either at your house or at the printers . . . I have always fancied you were a little harum-scarum and inaccurate now and then about the exact order and arrangement of sheets, pages and paragraphs . . . . That paragraph you so carelessly pasted over. I suppose that I must set to work to write something better if I can as a substitute. The same precisely I cannot recall. I think I should be able in a couple of days to do something. However, I should be deucedly inclined to swear at you I will allow."[11]

Finally it was done. Even the ongoing uncertainty of how to sign the finished manuscript was resolved. Clearly Ada wanted credit for her work, yet women did not write papers—certainly women of the nobility did not. Ultimately she decided to sign herself "A.A.L." Not quite anonymous, certainly not to her friends, but the identity of A.A.L. was kept secret from most people for some 30 years.

Now Lady Lovelace came into her own. She had proved herself Babbage's intellectual equal; one of her final letters of this period set down certain conditions aimed at avoiding strain and argument in any future collaboration between them. She wanted him to agree beforehand that any disputes that might arise from their differences of opinion would be submitted to a third party to be named beforehand. She wanted to ensure that their private relationship would not be damaged by any professional disagreement. In addition, if she was to continue placing her intellectual energies at his disposal she must get in return his individual help and attention when she needed it. Also, he must try to improve his work habits. "And can you promise" she writes, "not to slur and hurry things over, or to mislay, and allow confusion and mistakes to enter into documents, etc.?" And, at last: "I wonder if you will choose to retain the lady fairy in your service or not."[12]

Babbage did choose to do so. Somewhat under her spell he calls her "my dear and much admired Interpretess" and "Enchantress of Numbers". Fully appreciating the value of her work, he called her paper the best contemporary account of his machine. "These memoirs", he wrote, "taken together, furnish to those who are capable of understanding the reasoning, a complete demonstration that the whole of the development and operations of analysis are now capable of being executed by machinery."[13]

Of the seven notes Lady Lovelace included in her work, the first and the last are perhaps the most interesting. In Note A she made a detailed comparison between the Analytical Engine and the Difference Engine, showing the clear superiority of the former. "The Difference Engine can merely *tabulate* and is incapable of *developing*, the Analytical Engine can either *tabulate or develop*."[14] She also described how information was fed into the Analytical Engine on punched cards, very much as the Jacquard loom was programed to weave patterned fabrics. As in modern punch cards, the patterns of holes correspond to mathematical symbols. In Lady Lovelace's words, "We may say most aptly that the Analytical Engine *weaves algebraic patterns* just as the Jacquard loom weaves flowers and leaves."[15]

In another remarkable section Ada Lovelace predicts computer music. "Supposing, for instance," she writes, "that the fundamental relations of pitched sounds in the science of harmony and of musical composition were susceptible of such expression and adaptations, the engine might compose elaborate and scientific pieces of any degree of complexity or extent."[16]

The last note, is also fascinating. There Lady Lovelace cautions against overrating computers. Unlike some of the popular futurists of our own time, she understands the machine's limitations perfectly when she writes: "The Analytical Engine has no pretensions whatever to *originate* anything. It can do whatever we *know how to order it* to perform. It can *follow* analysis, but it has no power of *anticipating* any analytical revelations or truths. Its province is to assist us in making *available* what we are already acquainted with."[17] Any thinking which the machines do indeed do must be put in." They must be programed to think and cannot do so for themselves.

The Late Correspondence

The last stage of the correspondence between Ada Lovelace and Charles Babbage is entirely different again. These letters cover years of tragedy and failure for Babbage, years of scandal and failing health for Lady Lovelace. The two were involved together in testing mathematical theories of probability in a way which came close to ruining them both. They devised an "infallible system" to beat the odds at betting on horses.

Horses and horse racing had long been a passion with Lady Lovelace. For Babbage, their "system" offered hope and a solution to his ever-increasing financial difficulties. Most of his personal fortune had already been spent on the development of his still unfinished Difference Engine. The government had lost faith in the project's completion and had withdrawn its support. The correspondence of this period refers mysteriously to "the book", never named, which Babbage and Lovelace appeared to be passing back and forth between them. This was probably a code word for the betting system they had developed.

These adventures ended disastrously. Reality did not oblige by conforming to the probability estimates of these fine mathematicians. Unlike Babbage, Lady Lovelace was not wise enough to extricate herself before becoming badly in debt. She lost such large sums that she was forced to pawn the family jewels. She was to suffer pain and remorse over this, throughout the long illness which preceded her death from cancer several years later.

Her husband, who had himself been involved in the scheme initially, struggled along with Babbage to control her creditors and the mounting scandal surrounding her. Many of the lapses in the Lovelace-Babbage correspondence at this time probably result from Babbage's having destroyed, after her death, letters which he feared might damage her reputation.

An Epitaph

Ada Lovelace died of cancer in 1852, when she was just 36. At her own request, she was buried beside her father in Hucknall Torkard church in Nottinghamshire. Her contribution to mathematics was not so great or fundamental as her early promise had indicated. After her death the world forgot about Ada Lovelace. But as computers play a more and more vital role in modern science and technology, her work is being reexamined. As the first expositor of computer language and programming more than a century ago, she is now beginning to receive a more appropriate place in the history of mathematics and science.

From the Correspondence: a Game

In a letter dated February 16, 1840, Lady Lovelace wrote to Babbage describing a puzzle she has just discovered.

My dear Mr. Babbage

Have you ever seen a game, or rather puzzle, called Solitaire! There is an Octagonal Board, like the enclosed drawing (missing), with 37 little holes upon it in the position I have drawn them, & 37 little pegs to fill the little holes. One peg is abstracted to begin with, and then the remaining ones hop over & take each other. For instance if peg 19, the center one, is taken out to begin, then peg 6 may hop over peg 12 into the empty hole 19, & peg 12 is taken off the board; or peg 21 might hop over peg 20 into 19, & then peg 20 goes off the board. The pegs are only allowed to hop over each other at right angles, not diagonally. The puzzle is to leave only one on the board. People may try thousands of times and not succeed in this, leaving three, four, five, or many more even which have no neighbors to give them a lift off the board. I have done it by trying and observation and can now do it at any time, but I want to know if the problem admits of being put into a mathematical Formula, & solved in this manner. I am convinced myself that it does, though I cannot do it. There must be a definite principle, a compound, I imagine, of numerical & geometrical properties, on which the solution depends, & which can be put into symbolic language. I believe that much depends, to begin with, on the particular peg first abstracted, & am inclined to think there is but one which will admit of subsequent success. I believe these boards are to be had at every toy shop. I have numbered the holes in my drawing for the sake of convenience of reference. The real boards are not numbered.[18]

Figure 7-1 is a diagram of the board reconstructed from her description. (The drawing to which she refers in her letter is missing from the correspondence.) A game can be made by arranging the points on a large sheet of paper and covering them with beans, chips, checkers, or paper clips. Or a game board can be made by drilling holes in wood and using pegs or nails to mark and jump.

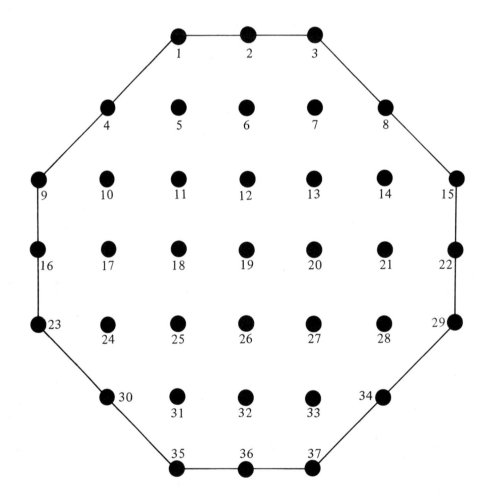

Figure 7-1. Game described by Lady Lovelace to Charles Babbage in letter of February 16, 1840.

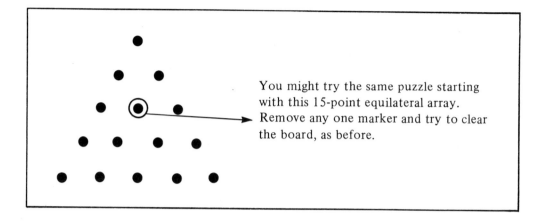

You might try the same puzzle starting with this 15-point equilateral array. Remove any one marker and try to clear the board, as before.

The last digit of the year of Ada Augusta Lovelace's birth is the third prime number.
The sum of the first and fourth digits is 6.
The sum of the second and third digits is 9.
The first and third digits are the same.

Ada Lovelace was born in the year ___ ___ ___ ___ .

Countess Lovelace was very young when she died.
Three of the four digits in the year of her death are the same as those in the year of her birth.
The last digit is the first prime number.

She died in the year ___ ___ ___ ___ .

Ada Byron Lovelace's Work

The Technique of Finite Differences

As she continued to study mathematics, Ada Lovelace began to look forward to the day when she would have enough background to work with Charles Babbage. She was so fascinated by his Difference Engine that the idea of "putting her mind at his disposal" became very important to her. Realizing that the method of finite differences was the key to the workings of the machine, she set out to understand the technique.

This section includes three activities and two games. Their solutions may be expressed as functions which can be evaluated by the method of finite differences. The plan for this section is as follows: first an activity or game will be introduced. Then solutions for simple cases will be derived directly from these activities. Finally, solutions for more complex cases will be found using the method of finite differences.

The Method in General

Here is how the method works. First look at Table 7-1. The function in Table 7-1 probably looks familiar. Row 1 is a list of counting numbers (n). Row 2 is a list of the squares of the numbers in row 1 $(f(n) = n^2)$. Fill in the missing numbers in row 2.

Table 7-1.

Row

		0	1	2	3	4	5	6	7	.	.	.
1	n	0	1	2	3	4	5	6	7	.	.	.
2	$f(n)=n^2$	0	1	4	—	16	—	—	—	.	.	.

These values may be extended as far as we wish, once it is clear that each value in the second row is equal to the number in the first row multiplied by itself. That is, if row 1 is *2* then row 2 is *2×2* or *4*. Table 7-2 shows Table 7-1 expanded to four rows. Look carefully at rows 3 and 4. Where do these values come from? Do you see how rows 3 and 4 are generated?

Table 7-2.

Row

		0	1	2	3	4	5	6	7	8	·	·
1	n	0	1	2	3	4	5	6	7	8	·	·
2	$f(n)$	0	1	4	9	16	25	36	49	64	·	·
3	$\Delta f(n)$		1	3	5	7	9	11	13	15	·	· ·
4	$\Delta\Delta f(n)$			2	2	2	2	2	2	2	· ·	· ·

Do you see that row 3 is a sequence of numbers which are the *differences* between pairs of adjacent numbers in row 2? This difference sequence is 1, 3, 5, 7, 9, 11, ...

Row 4 is another sequence. It is formed by differences between terms in row 3. Look at the differences in row 4. Notice that these differences do not change. For this function, these differences are always 2. Such a sequence of differences (2, 2, 2, 2, ...) is called a *constant* difference. This constant difference is the key to the working of the Difference Engine.

The Method and the Difference Engine

Suppose it is known that the constant difference for a particular function is *2* (row 4), but that the function itself is unknown. However, the first term of row 3 (the first difference sequence) is known. It is *1*. The first term of row 2 is also known. It is *0*. That is, *f(n)*=0 when *n*=0. Given enough time, the Difference Engine can then evaluate any *f(n)*. In doing this, it will use *addition* as the *only operation*. Since multiplication is merely repeated addition, all values may be obtained by addition alone.

Now try to perceive how the Difference Engine would view this problem. Complete the values of *f(n)* in Table 7-3 as the Difference Engine would do it. By adding the constant difference from row 4, complete row 3. Then complete row 2.

Table 7-3.

Row

		0	1	2	3	4	5	6	7	8	9	·
1	n	0	1	2	3	4	5	6	7	8	9	·
2	$f(n)$	0	1	4								·
3	$\Delta f(n)$		1	3								·
4	$\Delta\Delta f(n)$			2	2	2	2	2	2	2	2	· ·

Remember, the Difference Engine is unable to multiply. It can only add. Work from the bottom up. Start with the row of constant differences. Evaluate this function by addition alone.

Applying the Method

How many points? How many lines?

Start with *n* points on a circle. Find the maximum number of lines which can connect them. Call the number of points *n*. Call the number of connecting lines, *f(n)*. Figure 7-1 shows some simple cases.

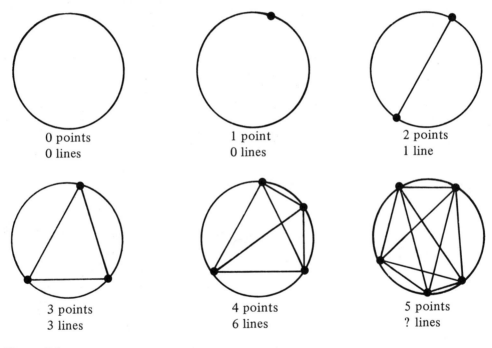

Figure 7-1.

Table 7-4.

Row

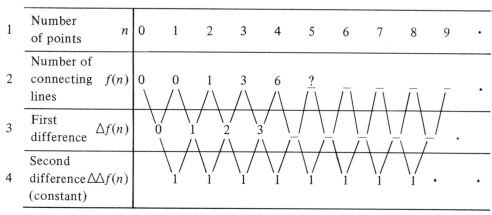

			n	0	1	2	3	4	5	6	7	8	9	·
1	Number of points													
2	Number of connecting lines	$f(n)$	0	0	1	3	6	?					·
3	First difference	$\Delta f(n)$		0	1	2	3						·
4	Second difference $\Delta\Delta f(n)$ (constant)			1	1	1	1	1	1	1	1	·	·

The constant difference for this function is *1* (row 4). Complete Table 7-4. Notice that the values in rows ③ and ② have been obtained from the experimental data above. Use Figure 7-2 to show solutions for some other cases.

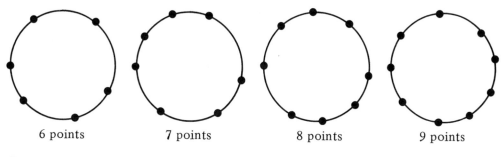

6 points   7 points   8 points   9 points

Figure 7-2.

You now know what the answer is for the more complicated situations. See Table 7-4, row 2; *f(n)* is the solution sequence.

Chop It

Find the maximum number of sections into which a region may be divided by any number of cuts. Call the number of cuts n. Call the maximum number of sections, $f(n)$.* Figure 7-3 shows some simple cases. Table 7-5 collects these data.

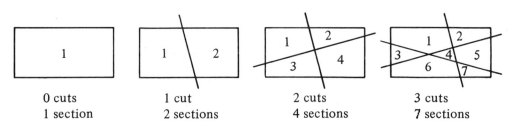

0 cuts	1 cut	2 cuts	3 cuts
1 section	2 sections	4 sections	7 sections

Figure 7-3.

Table 7-5.

Row

		n	0	1	2	3	4	5	6	7	8	9	.
1	Number of cuts												
2	Number of sections	$f(n)$	1	2	4	7							.
3	First difference	$\Delta f(n)$		1	2	3							.
4	Second difference $\Delta\Delta f(n)$ (constant)			1	1	1	1	1	1	1	1	.	.	

---

*Make certain that each new cut does not pass through the intersection of any preceding cuts—for example

This does not generate the maximum number of sections.

Run the machine. Complete Table 7-5.

Constant difference, row 4 = 1.

First entry, row 3 = 1.

First entry, row 2 = 1.

How many sections will you try to show with 4 cuts? How many sections will you try to show with 5 cuts? 6 cuts? 7 cuts? What about 8 cuts? 9 cuts?

Show *4* cuts.

Show *5* cuts.

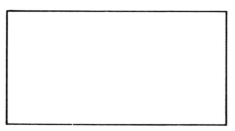

Show *6* cuts.

Show *7* cuts.

Figure 7-4.

Triangle Search

"Find triangles in a triangle." Find the maximum number of triangles with points "up" (△, not ▽) in a triangle built of triangular units. Call *n* the number of units along one edge. For example:

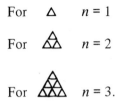

For   △ $n = 1$

For   <small>triangle figure</small> $n = 2$

For   <small>triangle figure</small> $n = 3$.

Call *f(n)* the number of "point up" triangles you may count in triangle *n*. Figure 7-5 shows some simple cases.

n	*f(n)*= total # of point up triangles.				Picture of *n*
0	0				
1	1	*1*	1=unit	△	▲
2	4	*3*	1-unit	△s	
		1	2=unit	△	
3	10	*6*	1=unit	△s	
		3	2=unit	△s	
		1	3=unit	△	
4	20	*10*	1=unit	△s	
		6	2=unit	△s	
		3	3=unit	△s	
		1	4=unit	△	
5	?	—	1=unit	△s	
		—	2=unit	△s	
		—	3=unit	△s	
		—	4=unit	△s	
		—	5=unit	△	

Figure 7-5.

Complete the information in Figure 7-5.*

---

*The grid in Appendix 6 may be reproduced and used for this activity.

Run the machine: Complete Table 7-6.

Constant difference (row 5) is 1.

First entry in row 4 is 2.

First entry in row 3 is 1.

First entry in row 2 is 1.

Table 7-6.

Row

		0	1	2	3	4	5	6	7	8	9	.
1	n	0	1	2	3	4	5	6	7	8	9	.
2	$f(n)$	0	1	4	10	20						.
3	$\Delta f(n)$	1	3	6	10							.
4	$\Delta\Delta f(n)$	2	3	4								
5	Con- stant difference $\Delta\Delta\Delta f(n)$	1	1	1	1	1	1	1	.	.	.	

Notice that this problem needed three difference sequences before the differences became constant. This means that the function which describes this activity would require the third power of n. It would be of the form an^3+bn^2+cn+d. See Appendix 7 for details.

Find more solutions. From your machine you know that there are _____ point up triangles in an $n = 5$ triangle. Can you find them? Use Figure 7-6. Can you actually locate all the point up triangles for $n = 6$? Can you find them for $n = 7$? $n = 8$?

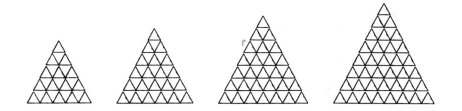

Figure 7-6.

Switch 'Em

This activity is a popular puzzle. Analysis shows that solutions for more and more complex cases may be churned out by the Difference Engine technique of constant (finite) differences.

Mark or cut out a strip with the required number of positions. Move two colors of paper, chips, or whatever, to try to solve the puzzle.

In Figure 7-7 find the minimum number of moves required for the red and blue markers to change places.

Figure 7-7.

The rules:
1. Reds move only to the right; blues move only to the left.
2. A proper move may be either a slide move into an empty space or a jump move over one marker into an empty space.
3. Red may jump over red *or* blue; blue may jump over blue *or* red.
4. Any color may move any number of successive times. The only restriction is on the direction of motion, as stated above.

The problem: Given a board of a certain size, find the minimum number of moves required to solve the puzzle. (All boards have an odd number of squares to accommodate an equal number of red and blue markers, and one blank space.)

Call the number of pieces of each color *n*.

Call the minimum number of moves *f(n)*.

Some simple cases are shown in Figure 7-9.

N: number markers of each color.	f(N): minimum number moves to trade Rs and Bs.	Picture of N
0	0	
1	3	R ▨ B
2	?	R R ▨ B B
3	?	R R R ▨ B B B
4	?	R R R R ▨ B B B B
5	?	R R R R R ▨ B B B B B
etc.		

Figure 7-8.

Run the Machine. Complete Table 7-7.

Remember, now 4 is the constant difference.

Data from simple cases will give the initial values to get started.

Table 7-7.

Row

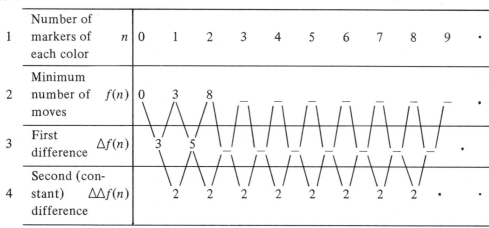

Notice that the constant difference for this puzzle is

The solution for $n = 4$ is _____ . Can you do the puzzle in that number of moves?

The solution for $n = 5$ is _____ . Can you do the puzzle in that number of moves?

Can you do the puzzle for six of each color? Seven?

Tic-Tac-Score! *

The Game:

The board: The game is played on an $n \times n$ grid.

The players: Two people play.

The play: Players alternate turns claiming squares on the board.

One player marks *O* in a claimed cell.

Other player marks *X* in a claimed cell.

The object: To score a maximum number of points.

The score: The player to mark the last cell in a row, column, or diagonal (which contains two or more cells) *scores 1 point for each cell marked* in that row, column, and/or diagonal.

At right are some examples on a 3 × 3 grid. Player A uses X's, Player B uses O's. The triangle indicates the most recent move.

Notice that the total score is 32. (21 + 11 = 32.)

Try another game. Notice that although the point distribution will vary from game to game, the total score for all games played on a 3 × 3 board will always be 32. Can you say why?

Now you know how the game is played. Let's explore the problem. The total *score* for each game is a number which *varies as* the *size of* the playing *board* varies. Given a board of any size, say $n \times n$ squares, the *total* score is always known. Call this number *f(n)*.

---

*This game was originally suggested by Mark Spikell.

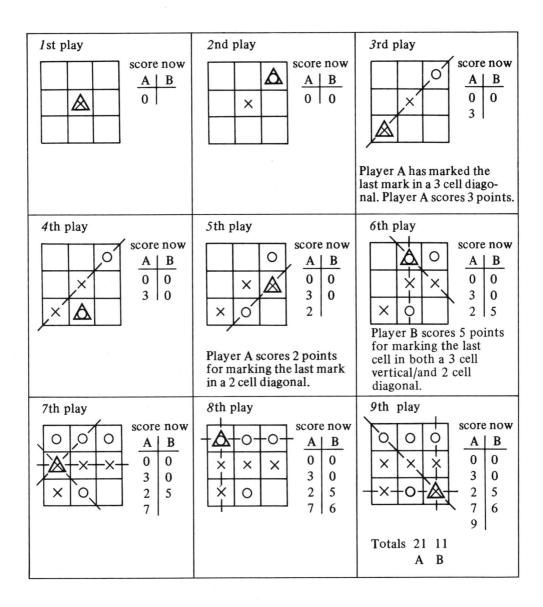

1st play

score now

A	B
0	

2nd play

score now

A	B
0	0

3rd play

score now

A	B
0	0
3	

Player A has marked the last mark in a 3 cell diagonal. Player A scores 3 points.

4th play

score now

A	B
0	0
3	0

5th play

score now

A	B
0	0
3	0
2	

Player A scores 2 points for marking the last mark in a 2 cell diagonal.

6th play

score now

A	B
0	0
3	0
2	5

Player B scores 5 points for marking the last cell in both a 3 cell vertical/and 2 cell diagonal.

7th play

score now

A	B
0	0
3	0
2	5
7	

8th play

score now

A	B
0	0
3	0
2	5
7	6

9th play

score now

A	B
0	0
3	0
2	5
7	6
9	

Totals 21 11

A   B

	n = size of $n \times n$ board	$f(n)$ = total score
1	□	0
2	⊞ Try this game. See if	12
3	you agree that the total score will be 12.	32
4		—
5		—
etc.		

Run the machine. Generate total scores for larger boards, filling in Table 7-8.
    The data: constant difference (row 4) is *8*.
               First entry in row 3 is *12*.
               First entry in row 2 is *0*.

Table 7-8.

Row

	Size of $n \times n$ board n	0	1	2	3	4	5	6	7	8	9	.
1												
2	Total score $f(n)$	0	12	32	—	—	—	—	—	—	—	.
3	First difference $\Delta f(n)$		12	20								.
4	Second (constant) difference $\Delta\Delta f(n)$			8	8	8	8	8	8	8	8	.

    Play the game on a 4 × 4 board. Can you verify the total score? Can you play and verify the scores for larger boards?[19]

The Functions Describe the Games

The following functions describe each of the activities we have worked with.

1. How many points?
   How many lines?

   $$f(n) = \frac{n(n-1)}{2} \qquad = \frac{1}{2}n^2 - \frac{1}{2}n$$

2. Chop it

   $$f(n) = \frac{n(n+1)}{2} + 1 = \frac{1}{2}n^2 + \frac{1}{2}n + 1$$

3. Triangle Search

   $$f(n) = \frac{n(n+1)\ (n+2)}{6} = \frac{1}{6}n^3 + \frac{1}{2}n^2 + \frac{1}{3}n$$

4. Switch 'Em

   $$f(n) = n(n+2) \qquad = n^2 + 2n$$

5. Tic-Tac-Score

   $$f(n) = 4n(n+2) \qquad = 4n^2 + 8n$$

See Appendix 7 for some related theory.

Sonya Kovalevskaya

1850–1891

In the middle of the nineteenth century Russia was a country trying to enter the machine age, much as England had done 100 years before. With broad support from the wealthy merchant class, peasants, and intelligentsia, Tsar Alexander II proclaimed the emancipation of the serfs in 1855. This act was to begin a new era of reform, considered essential before the country would be ready to move into the industrial age.

One of the principal targets for change was the educational system. Academic freedom was restored to universities, and higher education was encouraged. The universities were to be powerful movers in the liberalization of Russian life. At the very same time that many educational reforms were being instituted, however, the situation for women was becoming worse. In 1863 the Russian universities were closed to women.

The promise that the emancipation seemed to hold was short-lived. The powerful landowners were using every means at their disposal to restrict and circumvent the purposes of the new liberal reforms. Most of the peasants soon found themselves again in desperate circumstances, little or no better off than before their emancipation. Agitation for real change continued to be strongest among the intelligentsia. Much of it was centered in universities and student demonstrations.

This was Russia when Sonya Krukovsky Kovalevskaya was born in 1850. The middle child of a Russian family of the minor nobility, Sonya Kovalevskaya was to become one of the leading mathematicians of her time.

Her Early Years

A great deal is known about the life of this extraordinary and gifted woman. During her life an autobiographical account, *Recollections of Childhood*, was written and published in Russian. And shortly after her death her close friend, Swedish writer Anna Carlotta Leffler, fulfilled her part of a vow the two women had made each other—that when one of them died the survivor would write a biography of her. Together these two books provide a richly detailed picture of this fascinating, neurotic woman whose life was rocked by periods of intense triumph and despair. Throughout her life she alternated times of high productivity in mathematics or creative writing with complete ennui.

As a small child Sonya suffered from the feeling that she was the least loved of the three children in her family. Her sister Aniuta, six years older, enjoyed the special attention first children often receive. Her brother Fedya, three years younger, was the male heir that she herself had failed to be. Sonya seemed a nervous, withdrawn child, seldom called to be admired by guests as her brother and sister often were.

When Sonya was six years old, her father retired from his position as an artillery general. The family moved to their estate in Palobino. It was in this ancient feudal castle that Sonya grew up. The serfs had just recently been emancipated. As a member of the landholding class, her father felt a strong responsibility to attend carefully to the administration of his estates during this time of social unrest.

Sonya's mother was considered well educated for a woman of her class, but the upbringing of the young children was primarily the responsibility of the servants. Sonya's earliest years were spent in the care of a Russian nurse and a French governess, who were constantly in petty conflict. Soon after the family settled in the country, the parents decided that the children were not being raised properly. The Russian nurse was transferred to other household duties; the French governess was dismissed and replaced by an Englishwoman. Also at this time a Polish tutor was engaged for Fedya.

The new English governess, though herself the product of a Russian upbringing, set about to transform Sonya into a proper English "miss." Aniuta, considered a young adult at 15, escaped this treatment. At the same time however, this development meant that the girls were now separated much of the time. This separation was particularly difficult for Sonya, who had always adored her sister. Even worse, bad feelings arose between her governess and Aniuta; the Englishwoman seemed committed to isolating Sonya as much as possible from this sister, whom she considered an unsavory influence.

Sonya writes of the "modern" techniques of punishment which her new governess used. Instead of corporal punishment, she used psychological methods. Any misbehavior on Sonya's part was to be detailed on a sign pinned to Sonya's back and worn at dinner, where the entire family would see it. This punishment through humiliation was extremely painful for the sensitive little girl.

Sonya reports few bright moments in her years under the control of this Englishwoman. Education was an inhibiting and restricting process. Sonya's relationship with a paternal uncle Peter, whom she adored, was the exception. Uncle Peter often came to visit. Sonya was his favorite among the children. From him she was inspired with an early "reverence for mathematics, as for a very lofty and mysterious science, which opened out to those who consecrated themselves to it a new and wonderful world not to be attained by simple mortals."[1] Long before she was old enough to understand what her uncle was talking about, she experienced a feeling of wonder for mathematics as she sat on his knees and listened to him think aloud.

A story is told that when the family moved to the great country house, all the rooms were to be repapered as part of the general renovation. Because of an error, there wasn't enough wallpaper to cover one of the children's rooms. For several years this one room, Sonya's, was temporarily papered with some old lithographed lecture notes that had belonged to her father. These notes were from the calculus lectures of a prominent Russian mathematician.

> *These sheets, spotted over with strange, incomprehensible formulae, soon attracted my attention. I remember how, in my childhood, I passed whole hours before that mysterious wall, trying to decipher even a single phrase, and to discover the order in which the sheets ought to follow each other. By dint of prolonged and daily scrutiny, the external aspect of many among these formulae was fairly engraved on my memory, and even the text left a deep trace on my brain, although at the moment of reading it was incomprehensible to me.* [2]

Later, as a girl of 15 receiving her first lessons in differential calculus, in St. Petersburg, she astonished her teacher by the speed with which she grasped some of the ideas, "just as if I had known them before." [3]

When Sonya was 17, she and her sister became caught up in an idealistic movement for social reform among the Russian intelligentsia. The sisters were particularly interested in the role of women and in the limited educational opportunities then open to women in Russia. Just a few years before, in 1860, a liberal trend had been initiated at St. Petersburg University. New classes of students had been admitted to some lectures; women had been included among them. Yet these limited concessions did not include permission to take degrees. Then in 1862, following student demonstrations, the University had been closed. When it reopened the following year even these so-called liberties had been abolished. Nowhere in Russia was higher education open to women.

A Marriage of Convenience

Despite this turn of events, Sonya and her sister were determined to continue their studies. One way was open to them; although it was quite a radical solution, many of their young friends were choosing it. Since higher education for women was only possible abroad, and since young unmarried women from good families were not free to travel, the obvious solution was for these women to marry. So a style of marriages for "intellectual convenience" developed among these young people. All that was required was a willing male comrade. The girls found him in a young acquaintance of Aniuta's—the promising writer, translator, and student Vladimir Kovalevsky. He was in several ways associated with the current reform movement in Russia. Previously he had travelled abroad. In 1866 he had been a war correspondent for a Russian newspaper, reporting Garibaldi's liberation campaign in Italy. When the sisters proposed the marriage, the idea appealed to him; he was ready for a change. The only problem was that he wished to marry Sonya, not Aniuta. This was not a trivial problem! Although Vladimir was of good background and was likely to be acceptable to the Krukovskys, the family was shocked when they heard of the proposal. It was unthinkable that Sonya, the 18-year-old, should marry while her 23-year-old sister was still unmarried. The girls were immediately ordered back to Palobino. They were in despair.

At this point however, Sonya, the timid one, took matters into her own hands. She feigned elopement in order to force acceptance of the proposal. Without permission, she left home to visit Vladimir, a very unorthodox thing to do. In her absence she arranged to have a note delivered to her father telling him that she was going to be married. Krukovsky had no choice but to accept the engagement as a *fait accompli*, and he went immediately to fetch her back. The newly engaged couple was married shortly after.

The couple's first home was in St. Petersburg. There Sonya was introduced to Vladimir's political friends. During the six months they spent there Sonya continued to study a wide range of subjects. Her primary interest was mathematics, but she dreamed of a broad education which would include medicine and physics as well. Finally she realized that it was not possible to learn everything, that one life is barely sufficient to accomplish what one can in her chosen field. At this time the two decided to go abroad, Sonya to study higher mathematics and Vladimir, geology and paleontology.

Study Abroad

In the spring of 1869 they arrived in Heidelberg. Sonya remained there for two years, obtaining special permission to attend lectures at the University. Vladimir left after a few months to continue his studies elsewhere. Since theirs was still a marriage in name only, this separation had no more significance than any separation between friends. The purpose of the marriage—to make it possible for Sonya to travel and study abroad—had been achieved.

Sonya was the darling of her professors. They, along with the townspeople, were attracted by her shy, studious manner. "Soon the whole town was talking about the wonderful Russian student. People would stop to look at her in the streets and mothers would point her out to their children as an exemplary student."[4] At this time, Julia Lermontova came to live with her. Julia, the first Russian woman chemist, would receive a doctorate in 1874, along with Sonya.

In 1870 Sonya Kovalevskaya went to Berlin, where she hoped to study with Weierstrass, the great German mathematician. The university at Berlin was even more restrictive than Heidelberg. Women were not even allowed to attend lectures. No exceptions could be made. Sonya had originally approached Weierstrass with outstanding recommendations from her professors in Heidelberg. Skeptical, he had sent her away with a set of difficult problems, "convinced she would not succeed, and gave the matter no further thought." To his astonishment she returned the following week. Not only had the problems been solved correctly, "but the solutions were eminently clear and original."[5]

Weierstrass, powerless to modify the university restrictions on women students, offered to meet with her privately, generously sharing his lecture notes and his time. Sonya worked with Weierstrass for the next four years with the single-minded concentration which was to be characteristic of her productive periods. Personally, however, this was not a happy time for the young woman. The intensity with which she was working made her extremely nervous. Vladimir, who had completed his doctorate in paleontology at Jena, was now in Berlin. But Sonya was embarrassed by the circumstances of her marriage. Although Weierstrass and his family had accepted her very warmly, almost as a daughter and sister, she never introduced them to her husband or clarified to them her relationship with him.

In January of 1871, Sonya's studies were interrupted by an adventurous journey to Paris. Aniuta, who had been living there during the siege, had not been heard from recently. Hoping to discover what had happened to her, Sonya and Vladimir slipped into Paris on the eve of the Commune by commandeering a deserted rowboat on the shores of the Seine. They found Aniuta, and for a while the two women served in the ambulance corps, as bombs burst about the city.

Later, after she had returned to Berlin and her studies, Sonya was called to Paris once again. This time Sonya and Aniuta, together with their father (who by now had been told how Aniuta was living), completed their self-appointed mission to rescue Aniuta's lover, Victor Jaclard, from prison, where he had been sent for his revolutionary activities. Through his connections, General Krukovsky was able to help effect the young man's escape.

At the end of four years Sonya had produced three outstanding research papers. The first, on partial differential equations, was a remarkable contribution. Together these three papers qualified her for a doctorate from the University of Göttingen. Her contributions were so outstanding that the oral examination was waived when she petitioned that her German was inadequate. She received her degree in 1874.

Sonya and Vladimir, both with doctor's degrees, returned to Palobino in Russia. Aniuta and Jaclard, to whom she was now married, joined them there. For a while the entire family was reunited. Shortly after the reunion, however, the general

Marketplace, St. Petersburg, Russia, 1880. "Receiving a moderate inheritance upon her father's death, Sonya and Vladimir moved to St. Petersburg. There they entered into the whirl of social life ..."

died suddenly. Then, in her grief over her father's death, Sonya turned to Vladimir for consolation. Their marriage was finally consummated.

Receiving a moderate inheritance upon her father's death, Sonya and Vladimir moved to St. Petersburg. There they entered into the whirl of social life, which was elitist, fervently intellectual, and uniquely Russian. Their only child, a daughter, was born. Sonya did no mathematics during this time. She immersed herself completely in the life around her. This was a pattern which was to be repeated again and again throughout her life. Kovalevskaya's periods of work, either in mathematics or creative writing, were exceedingly intense and singleminded; her periods of relaxation were equally concentrated. Her moods also showed great contrast. She alternated periods of delirious happiness with deep despair.

Failure, Exile, and Vladimir's Death

At this time Sonya and Vladimir were involved in many financial ventures, all of them doomed to failure. In vain Sonya tried to rekindle her husband's excitement about science, at the same time hoping to deepen their personal relationship. She failed to do either. Vladimir was unable to get proper recognition for his work. One source says that Vladimir was made Professor of Paleontology at the University of Moscow in 1881. Others say that the promised appointment never materialized. Sonya also was doing poorly professionally. She was unable to find a suitable job. In Russia, women could only teach arithmetic in the junior grades of girls' schools. She was never invited to teach at the Bestuzhev Higher Courses for Women which had been opened in 1878, although it had been assumed that she would. She was probably considered to be politically unreliable—a dangerous nihilist, closely associated with radical circles. Whichever was the case, the situation in Russia was unsatisfactory both personally and professionally for the young woman.

In March 1881, when Alexander II was assassinated, the situation became even worse. Alexander's death brought on a wave of reaction against some of his relatively liberal reforms. Persons suspected of nihilist sympathies became targets for persecution. In this atmosphere any kind of scientific work was impossible. Leaving Vladimir in the control of his shady business associates, Sonya took their child and returned to Berlin.

There she once again threw herself singlemindedly into her work. Fufa, her daughter, was sent back to Russia after a scary illness. Sonya felt that she was living in an unsettled state and that the child would be better off in Russia with Julia.

At this time she received the shocking news of her husband's death. Faced with court proceedings when his business was accused of fraud, he had committed suicide. Sonya, inconsolable with guilt and grief, fell into a state of near collapse. After five days she regained her composure, and characteristically became more deeply immersed in mathematics than ever.

Sweden and Leffler

Finally, a position worthy of Sonya's talent became available. In Sweden, the University of Stockholm had just been established. Gosta Mittag-Leffler, an outstanding mathematician and a former student of Weierstrass was to form a mathematics department. He had heard of the work of the Russian woman and "...was eager to secure for his university the glory of attracting to it the first great woman mathematician."[6] Sonya was delighted with the offer, and, though it was temporary, she accepted.

Her arrival in Stockholm in November 1883 created great excitement in the press. One newspaper wrote, "Today we do not herald the arrival of some vulgar insignificant prince of noble blood. No, the Princess of Science, Madam Kovalevskaya, has honoured our city with her arrival. She is to be the first woman lecturer in all Sweden."[7]

She was popular with her students and generally; it became quite fashionable for parents to name newborn girls Sonya. After her success in the first year, Leffler was able to arrange a five-year appointment for her. Though she generally enjoyed wide support, all opposition had not yet ceased. The Swedish writer August Strindberg was a strong opponent of women's rights. In an article he supposedly proved "as decidedly as that two and two make four, what a monstrosity is a woman who is a professor of mathematics, and how unnecessary, injurious, and out of place she is."[8] On seeing the piece, Sonya sarcastically replied ... "only I wish he would prove clearly that there are plenty of mathematicians in Sweden better than I am, and that it was only *galantrie* which made them select me!"[9] Despite such attacks, Leffler was able to get a tenured position for her at the end of the five-year appointment.

By now, however, Sonya's early pleasure with Sweden had ended; she was restless. Stockholm was too provincial. It lacked the stimulation, both professional and intellectual, that she needed and seemed to find in other European cities. She particularly adored Paris and tried to return there as frequently as she could. She dreaded the extreme Swedish climate with its endless summer days and winter nights. For a while her daughter came to live with her again. As before, though, Sonya sent her back to Russia after a while. Sonya felt a conflict between her duties as a mother and official personage, as a woman and as a breadwinner.

Julia says, among other things, that many people will accuse me of indifference to my child. I suppose that is quite possible, but I confess that I do not care in the least for that argument. I am quite willing to submit to the judgment of the Stockholm ladies in all that has to do with the minor details of life; but in serious questions, especially when I do not act in my own interests, but those of my child, I consider it would be unpardonable weakness on my part were I to let the shadow of a wish to play the part of a good mother in the eyes of Stockholm petticoats influence me in the least. [10]

During this period Aniuta became seriously ill—an illness which was to go on for a long time, and which brought Sonya back to Russia many times. Aniuta finally died unexpectedly in 1887 in Paris, where she had gone for an operation which was to restore her health. Her death was a severe blow to Sonya, who had always adored her older sister.

Back in Sweden, Sonya continued to alternate periods of intense mathematical and literary creativity. Much of her literary work was done in collaboration with Anna Carlotta Leffler, sister of her close friend Mittag-Leffler and the author of Kovalevskaya's biography.

A Great Award and a Tempestuous Affair

In 1888 Kovalevskaya achieved her greatest professional triumph when she was awarded the Prix Bordin by the French Academy of Science for her paper *On the Rotation of a Solid Body about a Fixed Point.* The paper had been judged so exceptional that the prize money had been raised from 3000 to 5000 francs.

Sonya was now the toast of Paris, the belle of the academic communities of Europe. Her teacher Weierstrass was overjoyed by her success. He wrote, "I do not need to tell you how much your success had rejoiced my heart . . . as well as all your friends here. I have particularly experienced a real satisfaction; competent judges have now given their verdict that my faithful pupil, my 'weakness' is not a frivolous marionette."[11]

At the same time she was involved in a tempestuous love affair with a Russian compatriot whom she adored. Maxim is variously described as a prominent lawyer or the eminent Russian historian, whom she met when he came to lecture at Stockholm University in 1888 after he had been discharged from Moscow University for criticizing Russian constitutional law. Her Maxim was with her in Paris at the award ceremonies. But their relationship was never a peaceful one.

Their basic trouble was that they could not live together. For instance, in the summer recess of 1888 they both were occupied with different tasks. Maxim had to go to his Ukrainian estate on business, while Sonya had to complete her research work. He was displeased because Sonya could leave him for her studies at any moment. When Kovalevskaya became a Bordin Laureate, she remarked bitterly that a famous actress could be far more attractive to a man than a woman who studied till her eyes got swollen.[12]

Some accounts imply that much of the conflict between them was because Maxim wanted her to give up her work, to be merely his wife. This was obviously impossible for her now. More likely a problem arose about where they should live. Maxim had an appointment in Paris. Sonya was reluctant to give up her hard-won position in Sweden to join him there permanently. Neither one of them could return to adequate employment in Russia either. However this might have been resolved, a happy ending was not to be. Now, at the time of her greatest triumph, Sonya turned again to her writing in the deepest despair. During the summer in France she finished writing *Recollections of Childhood*.

The End of an Extraordinary Woman

In September of 1889 Sonya Kovalevskaya returned to her duties in Stockholm, completely dejected. She had always been extremely temperamental, experiencing bottomless depressions. This time seemed even worse, as though she had lost the will to live. Through exhaustion and mindless carelessness she contracted pneumonia, which was to be the cause of her sudden death in 1891. At the time of her death she was only 41 years old.

Sonya Kovalevskaya had been an extraordinarily versatile and talented woman. With the greatest of ease she could turn from a lecture on Abel's functions, to research on Saturn's rings, to the writing of verse in French or a novel in Russian or a play in Swedish, to sewing a lace collar for her little daughter Fufi. In reply to a friend's surprise at her involvement in literature as well as mathematics, she wrote,

Many who have never had an opportunity of knowing any more about mathematics confound it with arithmetic and consider it an arid science. In reality however, it is a science which requires a great amount of imagination, and one of the leading mathematicians of our century states the case quite correctly when he says that it is impossible to be a mathematician without being a poet in soul.... one must renounce the ancient prejudice that a poet must invent something that does not exist, that imagination and invention are identical. It seems to me that the poet has only to perceive that which others do not perceive, to look deeper than others look. And the mathematician must do the same thing.[13]

At the time of her death, Sonya Kovalevskaya was at the very height of her fame. By penetrating deeply into the methods of mathematical research, she had made brilliant discoveries. Her contributions are considered equal to those of any mathematician of her day by any of her colleagues who are qualified to judge.

Yet Sonya Kovalevskaya's story, in the final analysis, seems a very sad one. Liberated as she was for her time, she was still very much a product of her time. Never did she succeed in resolving her image of herself as a woman with her role as a productive, creative human being.

Sonya Kovalevskaya lived her life completely in the century named by the eighth prime number.

The sum of the middle two digits of the year of her birth is the sixth prime number.

The sum of the second and third digits of the year of her death is the seventh prime number.

The number of years she lived is the thirteenth prime number.

The first and fourth digits of the year of her death are the same.

Sonya Kovalevskaya lived from __ __ __ __ to __ __ __ __ .

Sonya Kovalevskaya's Work

The Puzzles of Infinity

Zeno's Paradox

Zeno was a Greek philosopher who lived about 450 B.C. One famous paradox attributed to him asks the question, "Could a runner ever get from A to B?"

A •————————————• • •
A   C   D   B

Obviously not! First he must run half the distance, to C. Then he must run half the remaining distance, to D. Then half of the remaining half. Then half of the still remaining half, and so on ... forever. Obviously he can never reach B. Yet he does reach B!

The solution to the paradox lies in the paradoxical idea that an infinite sequence may have a finite sum.

What does this have to do with Sonya Kovalevskaya? The behavior of these kinds of infinite sequences was of great concern to the nineteenth-century mathematical school of which she was a part. We will explore these sequences in this section.

What Is a Sequence?

The *counting numbers* are a sequence   (1) 1, 2, 3,   4, . . ., n, . . .
The *even* numbers are a sequence.   (2) 2, 4, 6,   8, . . ., $2n$, . . .
The *square* numbers are a sequence.   (3) 1, 4, 9,   16, . . ., n^2, . . .
The *triangular* numbers are a sequence.   (4) 1, 3, 6,   10, . . . $\dfrac{n(n+1)}{2}$, . . .

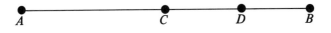

Mathematicians use the word *sequence* when values are listed in order according to some rule of formation. The dots in each sequence mean that the pattern continues.

How May a Sequence Behave?

Sequences (1), (2), (3), and (4) are of the same type. Each term in these sequences is larger than the one before. Not all sequences behave this way. Look at sequence (5).

(5) $+1, -1, +1, -1, +1, \ldots, +1, -1, \ldots$

This sequence does not behave the same way. No matter how far it is extended, its terms will continually oscillate between $+1$ and -1.

There are other kinds of sequences as well. Look at sequences (6) and (7).

(6) $1/2, 1/4, 1/8, 1/16, 1/32, \ldots 1/2^n$

Sequence (6) can be visualized easily as parts of a square.

(6)
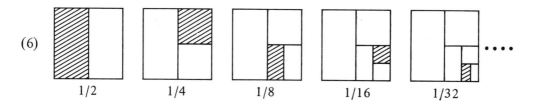

$$1/2 \qquad 1/4 \qquad 1/8 \qquad 1/16 \qquad 1/32$$

If each term in sequence (6) is added to the one before, we get another sequence which looks like (7).

(7)
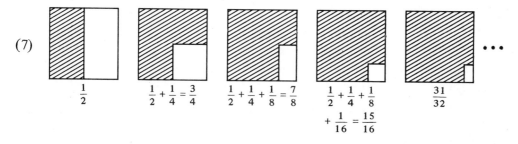

$$\frac{1}{2} \qquad \frac{1}{2}+\frac{1}{4}=\frac{3}{4} \qquad \frac{1}{2}+\frac{1}{4}+\frac{1}{8}=\frac{7}{8} \qquad \frac{1}{2}+\frac{1}{4}+\frac{1}{8} \qquad \frac{31}{32}$$
$$+\frac{1}{16}=\frac{15}{16}$$

Sequence (7), then, is the sum of the terms of sequence (6). We say that the terms of sequence (7) are approaching a limit. This limit is one whole square. We call sequences (6) and (7) *convergent sequences* since they approach a limit.

Since each term in sequence (6) may be thought of as the part which Zeno's runner has yet to run, we can think of sequence (6) as the sequence generated by Zeno's paradox. Sequence (7) shows the part of the total which Zeno's runner has already covered.

Some Other Sequences

Many activities generate infinite sequences. Some of these sequences are convergent, some are not. Some activities generate both convergent and non-convergent sequences. We will look at some here.

Disks of Gold

An ancient Hindu legend predicts the end of the world when the attending priests complete the task set for them by the god Brahma. Incessantly they continue their work—the transfer of sixty-four gold disks, one by one, from the first golden post to the third, according to the ancient rules. When the transfer is complete, the world will vanish!

Try a simplified version of this activity and you will realize that there is little cause for worry, even if the legend *is* true.

Start with 3 similar objects of different sizes. Three different coins would be perfect. Place them in a pile in order of size (smallest on top), on the first position of a board with 3 positions.

Three coins would look like this.

Three gold disks would look like this.

The object of the puzzle is to transfer the disks from the first post to the third post, in the minimum number of moves. But at no time may a larger disk be placed on a smaller one. See Figure 8-1 for the moves involved with three disks. The minimum number of moves is a function of the number of disks with which one starts.

Fill in Table 8-1.

Table 8-1

Number of disks n	Minimum number of moves $f(n)$
0	0
1	1
2	3
3	7
4	—
5	—
6	—

Analysis of moves for 3 disks

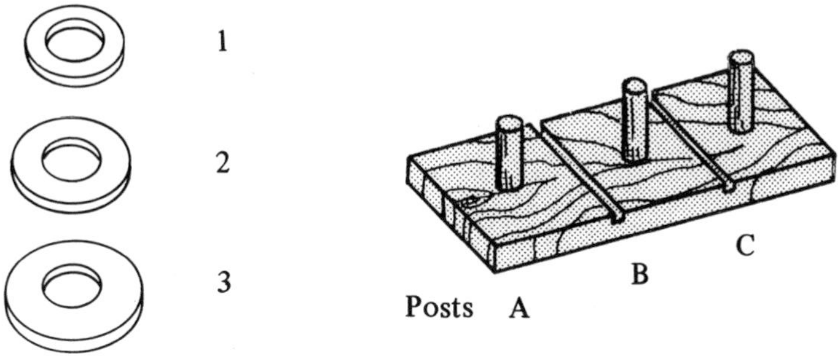

Disks

1

2

3

Posts   A   B   C

1		
2		
3		
A	B	C

(1)

2		
3	1	
A	B	C

(2)

3	2	1
A	B	C

(3)

	1	
3	2	
A	B	C

(4)

	1	
	2	3
A	B	C

(5)

1	2	3
A	B	C

(6)

	2	
1	3	
A	B	C

(7)

	1	
	2	
	3	
A	B	C

Figure 8-1.

Notice that the values of $f(x)$ increase rapidly. This function generates a non-convergent sequence.

Fold and Cut

Another activity generates exactly the same sequence, but is much easier to see. Try it if you are having disk transfer problems. It will help fill in Table 8-1.

Fold a sheet of paper twice. Cut the folded corner. Open the paper. How many holes?

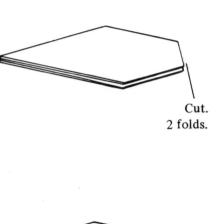

Refold the paper the way it was before. Then fold it over one more time. Again cut the folded corner. How many holes in the paper now?

Cut.
2 folds.

Continue to fold and cut. n is now number of folds; $f(n)$ is now number of holes.

The functions describing the disk transfer and the paper folding and cutting are essentially the same. The function for the disk transfer problem is $f(n) = 2^n - 1$; The function for the paper folding and cut problem is $f(n) = 2^{n-1} - 1$.

Cut.
3 folds.

Can you get some feeling for the enormous size of $2^{64} - 1$, the minimum number of moves needed to transfer 64 disks? If one disk were moved every second, the function says it would take 500,000 million years to transfer 64 disks.

Fibonacci and His Sequence

A fascinating number sequence that seems to occur over and over again in nature was first described by a thirteenth-century Italian mathematician, Leonardo Fibonacci. It is called the Fibonacci sequence in his honor. This sequence itself is not convergent. However, the *ratio between* each *adjacent pair* of terms in the sequence *does converge* to a famous proportion sometimes called the "divine proportion" or the "golden ratio."

The rule of formation of the Fibonacci sequence is simple. See if you can discover it. Complete the missing values when you do.

1, 1, 2, 3, 5, 8,___, 21,___, 55,___,___,___,___, ...

The sequence generated by the ratios of successive terms in the Fibonacci sequence converges towards 1.618034. . . . If we calculate several of these ratios we can watch them approach this value.

Fill in the missing terms in Table 8-2 and watch the process.

Table 8-2.

Adjacent terms $f(n), f(n-1)$	Sequence of ratios between adjacent terms $f(n) \div f(n-1)$
2,1	$2 \div 1 = 2$
3,2	$3 \div 2 = 1.5$
5,3	$5 \div 3 = 1.66$
8,5	$8 \div 5 = 1.60$
___,8	___ $\div 8 =$ ___
21,___	$21 \div$ ___ $=$ ___
___,21	___ $\div 21 =$ ___
55,___	$55 \div$ ___ $=$ ___
___,55	___ $\div 55 =$ ___
___,___	___ $\div$ ___ $=$ ___
___,___	___ $\div$ ___ $=$ ___
___,___	___ $\div$ ___ $=$ ___

Notice that these ratios oscillate and cluster closer and closer to 1.618034 . . . They actually approach the value $\dfrac{1+\sqrt{5}}{2}$.

The "Golden Rectangle"

The "golden rectangle" is a rectangle whose sides are related in a certain proportion. If a is the width and b the length, as in Figure 8-2, then $(a+b):b = b:a$. This ratio is called the "golden proportion."

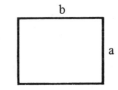

Figure 8-2.

     Geometrically, the golden proportion can be seen by forming rectangles whose dimensions are sums of squares of successive terms of the Fibonacci sequence. That is: $1^2, 2^2, 3^2, 5^2, 8^2, \ldots \ldots \ldots f(n)^2 \ldots$

    Figure 8-3 shows the growth of these golden rectangles. The shapes of these rectangles again approach the golden ratio. That is, the ratio of the dimensions of the sides of these rectangles approaches $\dfrac{1+\sqrt{5}}{2}$.

The sum of the squares		
1^2+1^2	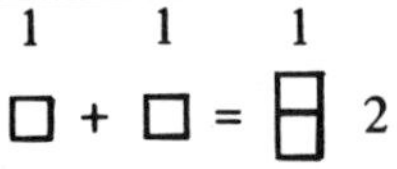 1 1 1 □ + □ = ▯ 2	proportion $2:1$
$1^2+1^2+2^2$	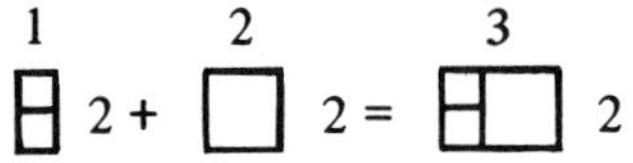 1 2 3 ▯ 2 + □ 2 = ▭ 2	proportion $3:2$
$1^2+1^2+2^2+3^2$	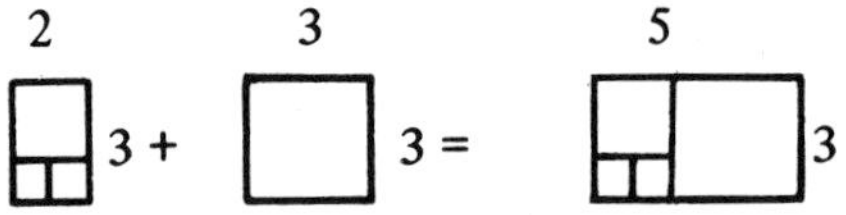 2 3 5 ▦ 3 + □ 3 = ▦ 3	proportion $5:3$
$1^2+1^2+2^2+3^2+5^2$	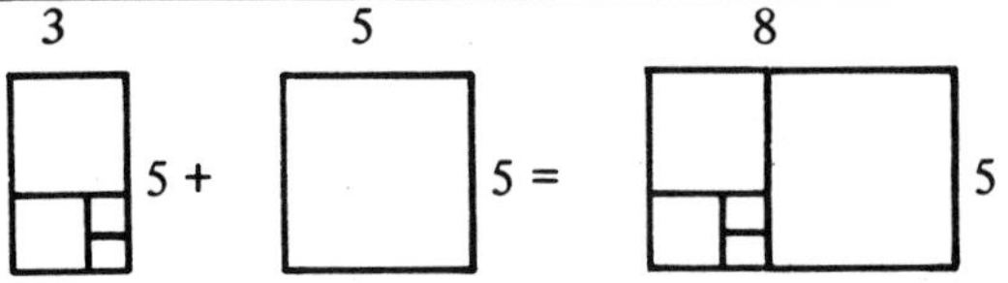 3 5 8 ▦ 5 + □ 5 = ▦ 5	proportion $8:5$

Figure 8-3.

We can reverse this process if we start with a golden rectangle and subtract squares instead of adding them. Each time the remaining rectangle will again be of "golden" proportion. Also, given the longer edge of a golden rectangle, say AC in Figure 8-4, point B (where $AB = AD$ and $ABED$ is a square) will divide AC in the golden proportion. That is, $AB{:}BC$ as $(AB{+}BC){:}AB= \dfrac{1{+}\sqrt{5}}{2}$. If we connect an arc through the successively smaller squares, the logarithmic spiral will appear.

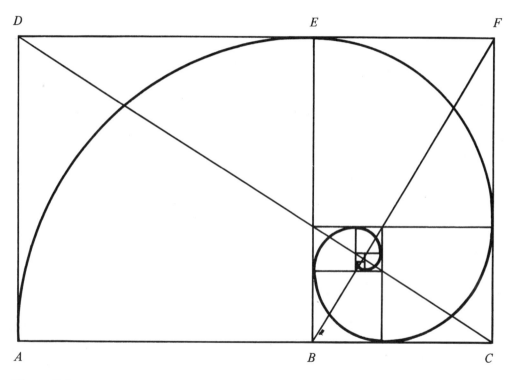

Figure 8-4.

The Pathological Snowflake

Another interesting example generates both convergent and nonconvergent properties at the same time. This figure, which "grows" according to a certain rule, is called the *snowflake*. It has the interesting property that its area converges to a finite quantity at the same time as its perimeter becomes infinitely large. Because of its "split personality," the snowflake is sometimes called the pathological curve.

The snowflake is generated in the following way:

1. Start with an equilateral triangle.
2. Divide each edge of this triangle into thirds. Build, off each middle third, another equilateral triangle of which the original middle third is one edge.
3. Continue this process *ad infinitum*.

The first three stages of this sequence will look like Figure 8-5.

Figure 8-5.

Figure 8-6 shows the first two stages of the snowflake as drawn on isometric paper (see Appendix 6). Try this yourself on the paper in Appendix 6. Continue the sequence of snowflakes at least until the fourth division.

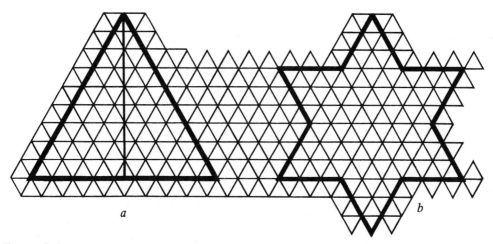

Figure 8-6.

Perhaps you can guess that the area will be limited to the size of the circle which would circumscribe the original snowflake triangle. The perimeter, on the other hand, becomes infinitely large. (See Appendix 8).

Grace Chisholm Young   1868–1944

Grace Chisholm Young was born in England in 1868, in the midst of Queen Victoria's reign. The Great Exhibition of 1851, set in the Crystal Palace at Hyde Park and designed to display the "Works of Industry of All Nations," had been a huge success. Modern technology was developing at an amazing rate, and Great Britain was the center of this world of technology.

Education in England, however, remained much as it had been during the lives of Mary Somerville and Ada Lovelace. Although some children were taught to read and write by their parents, at mid-century almost a third of the working poor were illiterate. As late as 1881, about 20 percent of the population still could not sign their names.

Not until 1870 was a law passed which made some sort of schooling available to every English child. By 1880, school attendance was compulsory; the age of leaving school was increased to 11, then 12, and finally, at the turn of the century, to 14.

For most women, education was still restricted to Bible reading and training in the homely arts. Mathematics and the classics were generally considered unsuitable subjects for women. The nineteenth century, however, was to see the beginning of pressure for reform. By the end of the century there were several excellent day schools and boarding schools for girls. In some of these, women were receiving educations which would qualify them for university entrance examinations. This was the situation in England when Grace Chisholm was born.

The Early Years

The youngest of four children, Grace Chisholm was born into a well-educated upper class family. In 1877, when she was still quite young, her father retired from his prestigious job as Warden of the Standards. He had been in charge of the Department of Weights and Measures of the British government. Grace, who was called "Baby" in the family, wrote warmly of her visits to her father's office when she was still very small.

Papa had his office at the Old Palace Yard, in the corner between the Houses of Parliament and Westminster Abbey. Baby loved the office and Mr. Chaney the chief clerk, and she always went there to see the Queen arrive in her grand carriage with her piebald horses and her gorgeous footmen. You saw the horses and the footmen and the coach but you hardly saw the dingy old Queen at all. [1]

Shortly before her father's retirement, Grace's family settled in Haslemere, a town outside London. There the children were raised. The family was prominent in the town: Grace's mother was an outstanding pianist, and with her husband she gave piano and violin recitals in the Haslemere Town Hall.

As a child Grace realized that her father was an important person. She adored him. The home contained many testimonials to his importance. "She looked every day at the ugly but gorgeous Sèvre vase in the corner of the drawing-room with its golden inscription from the grateful republic of France, and she danced with delight round the beautiful silver punch bowl with its silver lions . . . a present from the Czar of all the Russias."[2]

Grace was younger and freer than the other children in the family. As a young child she had been troubled by nightmares and headaches, and so, on the advice of the family doctor, her education was to be informal. She was to be taught only what she specifically asked to learn. The lessons she asked for were mental arithmetic and music. Since both these subjects were well within the expertise of her mother, Grace's education continued at home until she was 10 years old.

During this period she spent a great deal of time with her father. She writes about a trip to town when her father took her with him on some business to the Mint.

The Master of the Mint took the little girl all round, and she always remembers watching the automatic balance making up its mind as to whether a threepenny bit was right, or too light, or too heavy, and when it was certain, tipping it into the appropriate receptacle. He also showed her a row of big black books, and told her they called them "Chisholms" and that they were in constant use for reference at the Mint.[3]

Many pleasant hours were spent in her father's carpentry workshop, father and daughter working busily and happily side by side.

When Grace was 10 years old Mama put an end to the free running about, since "the child seemed to have given up screaming and walking in her sleep, although she was still subject to bad headaches."[4]

The difference in education for boys and girls in this family reflects the typical pattern for Grace's class and time in England. Hugh, her brother, had gone to a grammar school, then on to a prestigious boarding school. As an outstanding student he earned a first-rate scholarship to Oxford, where he was to continue a brilliant classical career. Her sister Helen, on the other hand, studied at home with a governess.

When Grace's mother had decided it was time to provide her younger daughter with some more formal education, she engaged a governess for her. This tutoring was Grace's only formal childhood education. Together with her natural ability, however, it was sufficient for her to pass the Cambridge Senior Examination when she was seventeen. Had she been a boy, the next step would have been to apply for university entrance. Since she was a woman, however, this was not considered. Instead, the family hoped to involve her in social work among the London poor, which was considered a more suitable way for educated young women to pass their time before marriage.

Grace Chisholm was determined to continue her studies, however. Her first choice, medicine, was forbidden by her mother. With the strong support of her father, however, she decided to study mathematics at Cambridge, which was then the mathematical center of England. She was able to win a prestigious scholarship to Girton College, one of the new Cambridge women's colleges. Her father matched the value of the scholarship, and in April, 1889, on her twenty-first birthday, she was off to the university.

Grace at Cambridge

At the time Grace Chisholm arrived at Cambridge, female undergraduates were at last being admitted, but formal degrees were still not being granted to women.

At Cambridge Grace Chisholm saw her future husband for the first time. William Young was a tutor at Girton College when Grace arrived there. In the English university system, tutors work closely with students and direct the details of their studies. At certain times, students take examinations. It is their standing on these examinations that determines the degree they are granted. These degrees are equivalent to grades, since class standing is determined by how well students do on the examinations for which they "sit."

Because of his reputation, Grace avoided William Young when she chose her own tutor. He was considered an excellent coach, a ruthlessly efficient and hard-working crammer, who could be very effective. Yet he was said to be sarcastic and to make his women students cry. Grace was afraid of him.

She writes of her first view of William Young outside the window of a friend's room one day. "She heard faintly the scrunch of the gravel and turned her head quickly to look. What she saw however was entirely unexpected. This dreaded Mr. Young, this great mathematical gun, was a boy, hardly older than herself."[5] For a year, while her regular tutor was on leave, Mr. Young was her tutor. No record exists of their interaction during that term, however; it does not appear to have seemed significant to either one of them at the time.

Although Cambridge was reputed to be the center of English mathematics while she was there, Grace Chisholm found it in a sorry state when she arrived. Arthur Cayley, as chief mathematician, was presiding over a subject which he considered "completely formed." "The atmosphere around him was stifling to the young mathematician." she writes. "Cayley, unconscious himself of the effect he was having on his entourage sat, like a figure of Buddha on its pedestal, dead-weight on the mathematical school of Cambridge."[6]

While tutors were the student's main faculty contact, the professors, like Cayley, lectured from time to time. In the middle of Grace's second term, her tutor suggested that she go to hear Cayley lecture. Grace was thrilled by the idea, but getting permission from her headmistress seemed a formidable task. She brought her friend Isabel Maddison to help her make her request. Permission was not given easily. Such a proposal from two first-year students was audacious, hardly worth consideration. But since the suggestion had come from their tutor, their headmistress reluctantly gave her permission. She wrote a note for them to take to Professor Cayley to ask if they could hear him lecture. After some difficulty, they found his house just as he was about to leave for his lecture. He was extremely cordial. "You are just in time," he said. "Follow me."

Grace Chisholm's description of the journey and lecture is delightful.

Grace and Isabel darted after him. It was a most amusing race. They were too afraid of losing sight of the swift moving professor to look at one another, or laugh. The flapping black gown sped ahead, across Trumpington Street, round a corner, in through a wicket gate and across a court, round another corner and, as the two girls hurried after, they beheld the tail of a gown whisking up a flight of stairs in a large building on the right. Up the stairs they flew and passed through an open door into a small lecture room. Professor Cayley, having already divested himself of his cap, was fumbling about the blackboard with the chalk and sponge. At the long table Mr. Berry was seated with another man in academicals, and the mathematical dons of Girton and Newnham were present in their everyday attire with hats.

"I was talking about polyacra," said Professor Cayley.

It was the beginning of a flow of words only to be likened to the flight of the great little man from Mill Lane to the lecture room. Grace's pen flew over the paper. Polyhedra with vertices constantly springing from triangular faces, like crystals growing in a solution, trees with branches forking in all directions succeeded one another without intermission, twining this way and that round the professorial head, or emerging from under his flapping sleeves as he stood with his back to the listeners chalking and talking at the same time at the blackboard. The lecture came to an end as suddenly as it had begun. The little man came to a period, gathered up his papers under his arm, caught up his cap and, bowing deeply to his audience, made off as fast as he could down the staircase. [7]

By 1893 Grace had taken both her final examinations and qualified for a first-class degree at Cambridge. At this time she had high hopes for a career as a mathematician. But despite her outstanding work at Cambridge, she could go no further there. Women were not yet admitted to graduate schools in England.

Grace at Göttingen

Göttingen, a pleasant little German university town, was considered at the time to be the major center for creative mathematics in Germany, and probably the world. Gauss had lived and worked in Göttingen. The leading mathematician there now was Felix Klein. He was to be Grace's advisor and close friend for many years to come.

By going to Göttingen, Grace Chisholm had chosen the right place at the right time. Professor Klein's reaction to her application was very cordial. As long as her qualifications were in order, he was delighted to support her. The final decision to admit her rested with the Berlin Ministry of Culture, but there also she was fortunate. The official in charge of higher education in Germany at that time was a remarkable liberal, Friedrich Althoff. He was particularly interested in supporting education for women.

So everything was arranged. Professor Klein was to be her advisor, and she and two other women were to be allowed to attend lectures. They were now finally graduate students, but being women students created special problems, some of which are amusing in retrospect. Grace wrote home that if they were early for lectures they were to wait in the sanctum, or professor's private room, "to avoid the students who loaf and lark in the corridors for a quarter of an hour after the nominal hour for lecture to begin. . . . Klein, instead of beginning with his usual 'Gentlemen!' began 'Listeners!' with a quaint smile: he forgot once or twice and dropped into 'Gentlemen' again, but afterwards he corrected himself with another smile."[8]

She writes about a first lecture she gave at Professor Klein's seminar. It is difficult not to empathize with her.

> *Once I had written some equations down and Professor Klein asked me to verify them as there seemed to be a discrepancy. Now I did not feel equal to doing any brain work then and there, and for one moment I had a pang of despair; but Dr. Ritter got up and explained that I had rubbed out a minus sign by mistake and I blessed him: that showed he was attending. Another time Professor Klein asked for an explanation of certain facts, a thing he is very fond of doing. I had been more frightened than anything of his questions, it is so difficult to think on an occasion like that, and although the same thing happens to nearly every one I always think it looks foolish not to be able to answer. The gods willed on this occasion that my brain should work, and I gave the explanation to my own astonishment, and, I fancy, to his too.*[9]

And so her experience at Göttingen was a gratifying one. She was treated with particular kindness by the Kleins. She met many people during visits to their home. Presently it was time for her to think about receiving a formal degree—an important precedent. Sonya Kovalevskaya had received a docterate from Göttingen, but she had

The Mathematics Club of Gottingen, 1902. Seated in the first row with Mrs. Young are Hilbert and Klein (third and fourth from the left).

been the first and her degree had been an informal one. Kovalevskaya had never actually attended the university itself, or been examined. When Grace brought the matter to Professor Klein's attention, he was again very supportive. "He had evidently been thinking it all out himself and was just waiting for me to speak. He says it is his opinion that the admission to the examination and doctorate is a matter only for the consideration of the Faculty. Nothing is said in the charter about the recipients being men, simply because such a thing was never dreamt of. It might be necessary to request government permission . . . but he did not anticipate any problem and was planning to bring the matter to the attention of the faculty.[10]

As expected, everything proceeded smoothly. Government approval was wholeheartedly granted. Now the final oral examinations were all that remained for Grace to complete. An amusing incident relates to this. She writes that she had ordered a carriage in time to take her to the examination. I ". . . was sitting in the window (waiting) for the carriage to drive up, when to my surprise I saw a carriage drive away from my house. [I thought] he must be going to turn round, but instead of that it drove away." Looking at her watch she realized she was going to be late. Checking with the maid it turned out the carriage driver *had* called at the house to ask for the *gentleman* who had ordered the carriage. He had assumed it was a gentleman since he was told he was bringing someone to take a doctoral examination. The maid had sent him away. There was no gentleman in the house. "I had to go on my legs as fast as I could, and of course I lost my way, but after wandering round several triangles and squares I got to the Aula very hot and five minutes late."[11] But no one was quite ready, so no harm had been done.

The examination went well, and then it was over. She was a doctor—the first official doctorate granted a woman in Germany in any subject whatever. "I was almost stupified," she wrote. She was presented with an exquisite bouquet of flowers from one of the professors. "The next moment Miss Winston [a friend and colleague] arrived; we used the occasion to execute a war dance of triumph. Then the professors came congratulating and beaming."[12]

Marriage and Family

Grace returned to England. As was customary, her dissertation was reproduced and copies were sent to people to whom it might be of interest. One was sent to her former tutor, William Young. In the fall of that year he wrote to thank her for her paper and suggested a collaboration on an astronomy book. Thus they began to see each other again.

The story Grace tells about the incident in which Young proposed marriage seems to summarize their entire relationship. Aware only of his own needs and desires, William Young seemed to have had a great capacity for riding roughshod over people.

Although his energy, vitality, and enthusiasm were boundless, he sapped others. During their long marriage and frequent collaborations, he drained much of his wife's strength. So demanding was he that when he would leave on one of his frequent, prolonged absences from the family, it is said that Grace would go to bed for days with a sick headache. After three days in bed she would be up and functioning again. This seemed to be her way of regaining control of herself.

When he first asked Grace to marry him she refused, saying that she could neither marry him nor anyone else. But he didn't hear her. Soon after, she fell in love with him, and it was never necessary that she disillusion him. They were married in London in June of 1896 and lived at Cambridge their first year together. William continued his teaching there, supporting them adequately. Grace was free to continue her research and writing.

At the end of that year their first child, a boy, was born. At this time the Youngs decided to move to Germany. They felt that the great emphasis at the English universities on preparations for examinations, stifled the free exchange of ideas, and the atmosphere at the universities was no longer congenial to creative research.

Their next years seem completely out of step with their time. In many ways their existence was an extremely Bohemian one. They lived far removed from family and the strictures of the English society in which they had grown up. Both Grace and William were committed to their work and were productive by the standards of their peers.

Grace wrote of the year they spent in Italy in 1898. "Bimbo," the baby, occupied much of her time. "At the little hotels where we put up, baby slept contentedly in a drawer on his own bedding which we had brought. I carried him everywhere myself, and wherever I passed I heard the people say, in one dialect or another: 'What a lovely child!' "[13] Bimbo was a beautiful child: he looked like an angel but behaved very much like a child.

Grace wrote about the trials of raising a fifteen-month-old. In Turin, "one day, having left my husband in bed and Bimbo contentedly playing, I came home from the University to find a great to-do in our court. The porter seized me with voluble complaints; but I did not need his explanation, I could see for myself. On our balcony stood the angelic Bimbo armed with missiles of coal, which he was hurling down on anyone who ventured underneath."[14]

Returning home from one prolonged trip they were greeted with news of the baby who was well and jolly . . . and could now "count from *uno* up to *dieci*, only he usually left out *sette*."[15]

A Mathematical Union

The picture of Grace Chisholm Young's life which gradually emerges is a fascinating one. Doubtless she was a woman of tremendous energy and very much a part of the time in which she lived. Yet she also seems very contemporary. Her work was always very important to her, and she continued during much of her life to be productive and creative. It is difficult to sort out how much of their collaboration is due to her and how much to her husband. Their collaboration was extensive. (In 1906, for example, they jointly published the first textbook on set theory, a classic work in its field.) From their letters we suspect that Grace was responsible for a greater share than she is usually credited with. In one letter Grace is referred to as "the catalyst." Through her, his "flood of ideas" is refined! Another letter from Will to Grace, written during one of their many separations, seems to indicate that he knew how great her contribution was to their collaboration.

I hope you enjoy this working for me. On the whole I think it is, at present at any rate, quite as it should be, seeing that we are responsible only to ourselves as to division of laurels. The work is not of a character to cause conflicting claims. I am very happy that you are getting on with the ideas. I feel partly as if I were teaching you, and setting you problems which I could not quite do myself but could enable you to. Then again I think of myself as like Klein, furnishing the steam required—the initiative, the guidance. But I feel confident too that we are rising together to new heights. You do need a good deal of criticism when you are at your best, and in your best working vein.

The fact is that our papers ought to be published under our joint names, but if this were done neither of us get the benefit of it. No. Mine the laurels now and the knowledge. Yours the knowledge only. Everything under my name now, and later when the loaves and fishes are no more procurable in that way, everything or much under your name.

There is my programme. At present you can't undertake a public career. You have your children. I can and do.[16]

Altogether there were six children within the nine years from 1897 to 1908. During this time the family was living in Göttingen. While the children were young, one or the other of Will's unmarried sisters lived with Grace and the children. This special help made it possible for Grace to continue her studies, research, and writing, as well as to join Will abroad from time to time.

Will never succeeded in obtaining a permanent academic position, and he was away from the family for large parts of the year. The entire time the children were being raised, the family lived in temporary homes, waiting for the time when they would finally settle down. That time was never to come. Although Will was an outstandingly productive mathematician and was president first of the London Mathematical Society and later of the International Mathematics Union, he never seemed to be the right person for the few first-rate professorships which became available. Grace of course was never considered, neither by the world nor by herself. Being a mother of so large a family clearly prohibited any formal commitments outside the home.

With all the hectic activity involved in raising her family, often with no help, Grace was marvelous. She was closely involved with the education of her children, and her creativity showed itself here too. To teach Bimbo biology, she wrote a small book describing the principles of cell division in a short story which began with storks on top of a house they had once seen. It was called *Bimbo* and was published in 1905. A book on geometry through paper folding, written in collaboration with Will, was also published that same year. Although it was not well received originally, it has recently been reissued and seems extremely contemporary now.

The children turned out splendidly. Frank (Bimbo), who was killed in World War I, had shown great promise as a scientist. Through two of her daughters Grace was able to achieve some of her unfulfilled dreams. Janet became the physician Grace had always wanted to be. Another daughter, Cecily, took a doctorate in mathematics at Grace's college at Cambridge and received a fellowship, which Grace had failed to do. Even in 1929, however, Cecily was not able to receive a formal degree from Cambridge; degrees were not yet being granted to women at Cambridge, though Göttingen had been doing so for many years. Laurie, the eldest living son, became a mathematician also. Pat, the youngest son, became an outstanding chemist.

Grace and William Young's return to England, precipitated by the beginning of World War II, didn't happen as planned. As the situation on the Continent deteriorated, Grace made arrangements to return. Will, paranoid about English reaction to his long-standing German sympathies, refused to go with her. Grace finally left for England alone. Then France suddenly fell, and the plan for Will to follow was aborted. In the summer of 1942, when they had been separated for two years, Will died suddenly, a few days before his seventy-ninth birthday.

Grace spent her last years living with her daughter Janet and caring for her grandchildren. She died in 1944, shortly after her seventy-sixth birthday. A proposal granting her a rare honorary fellowship at Girton College was awaiting approval at the time.

The story of Grace Chisholm Young is particularly relevant to this book, because it raises some interesting questions. Are women capable of being creative mathematicians? Or is this a gift given only to men, as Mary Somerville seemed to think?

In Grace and William Young we see two careers which might suggest answers to these questions. Much of the work these two people did was in collaboration. How was credit sorted out? Was Will more creative than Grace? Was Grace not creative at all?

Grace had been considered a brilliant research mathematician as a student at Cambridge. Will, an excellent teacher, had done no original research at that time. After marriage the two became involved in many collaborations. Suddenly, at the unusually late age of 35, Will emerged as the creative mathematician. Grace proceeded to produce six babies in nine years and was no longer considered her husband's equal as a mathematician. Ideas supposedly poured from him, generally during periods when he was working abroad, sheltered from the turmoil which is an inescapable characteristic of households with young children. Even then, however, his ideas were first sifted and sorted by Grace before they took shape, again through her discipline, into solid publishable work.

Besides Grace's more intense immersion in the life of a household overrun by children, and the problems involved in settling and resettling her family often in foreign countries, the periods when Will was with the family created additional drains on her energy. "When Will was at home he completely monopolized Grace's life and duties. He knew that he was making excessive demands on her, but he could not help himself and realized that one of the advantages of his travels was that it would give Grace periods of quiet and undisturbed work."[17] When Will was in India in 1914, heading a department of mathematics at the University of Calcutta, Grace—who had not published a paper alone since 1905—started publishing a series of papers on the foundations of the differential calculus. This culminated in 1915 with a long essay which won her the Gamble Prize at Cambridge. Again we see her productivity emerging, but only when Will was far away.

When Will Young first proposed marriage to her, Grace's initial reaction was negative. Clearly she was aware of what marriage, especially at that time, would mean to her dreams of doing mathematics. As things turned out, she succeeded remarkably well at balancing work, marriage, and the raising of a large family. There is no way of knowing what she might have accomplished given the relative freedom of the men of her time. What we do know is that she produced a substantial amount of excellent work as a mathematician, while supporting a great deal more of her husband's work, and all the while raising six children who were to become distinguished adults.

The second and fourth digits of Grace Chisholm Young's birth year are the same. They are each 2^3.

The sum of the first and third digits is the fourth prime number.

Grace Young lived to be $[(7 \times 11) - 1]$ years old.

She lived from __ __ __ __ to __ __ __ __ .

Grace Chisholm Young's Work

From the First Book of Geometry

Grace Young's *First Book of Geometry*, originally published in 1905, has recently been reissued. The book looks surprisingly contemporary.

In the introduction Grace Young points out that solid geometry receives much less attention than plane geometry in primary and secondary schools. This is unfortunate, since "... in a certain sense Plane Geometry is more abstract than three-dimensional, or so-called Solid Geometry."[18] Since solid geometry is a more natural part of experience, it should be taught early. But it is very difficult to represent three-dimensional figures on a two-dimensional surface. In order to deal with the difficulties involved in demonstrating solid geometric concepts, Grace believed that students should make and handle three-dimensional figures. To provide this experience, she included many diagrams of three-dimensional figures in the book which were to be cut, folded and refolded. She believed students would in this way become familiar with the properties of these figures and would use them as aids in visualizing theorems in solid geometry. We include several patterns (or nets, as they are called) from her book.

Fold a cube

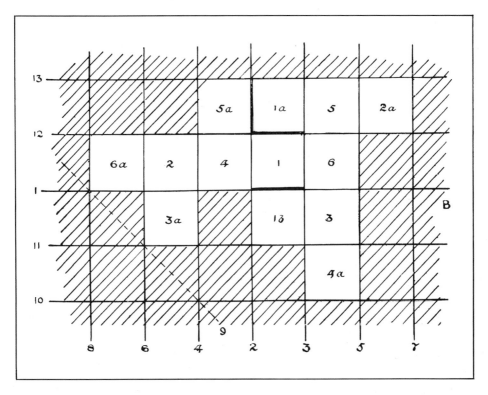

Figure 9-1. Cube

Cut along *all* heavy black lines and cut off all the shaded parts.

> ". . . *make a paper model of a cube . . . see that all your folds go the same way (. . . when you fold the paper along any one of them, the same side of the paper is the outside). Finally fit the model together by tucking the squares with the same number under one another, the letters in order showing which square comes above another; thus 5b comes above 5a, and 5 comes outside all the squares with the same figure.*"[19]

Fold a dissected cube

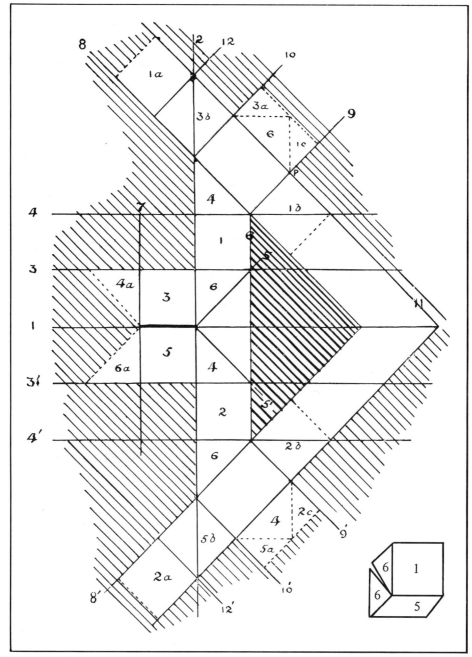

Figure 9-2. Dissection of a cube. This figure, when folded, forms a hinged model of a cube.

Figures with triangular faces

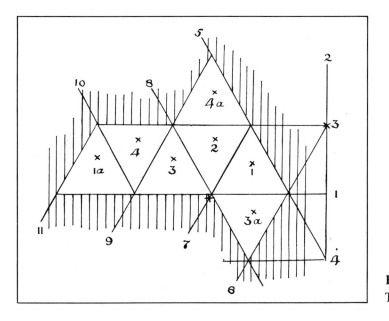

Figure 9-3.
Tetrahedron

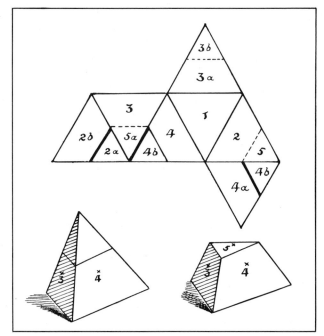

Figure 9-4.
Sliced tetrahedron

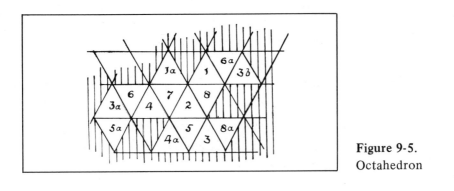

Figure 9-5.
Octahedron

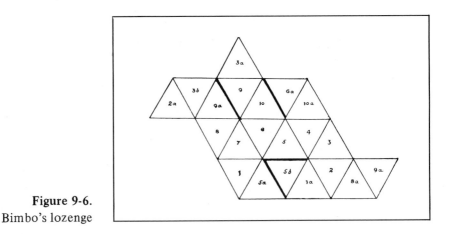

Figure 9-6.
Bimbo's lozenge

Enlarge these figures onto the isometric paper in Appendix 6. (A convenient enlargement will be 4 to 1, △ to △ .) Then cut and fold figures. The heavy lines indicate cuts. All other internal lines indicate folds. When folding figures, fold sections in order as discussed previously for folding a cube.

Using the assembled figures as references, complete Table 9-1. (See p. 79 for definitions of *edges, vertices,* and *faces*.

Table 9-1.

Figure	Number of edges (E)	Number of vertices (V)	Number of faces (F)
9-1			
9-2			
9-3			
9-4			
9-5			
9-6			

Can you discover a relation among E, V, and F? (This is the famous Euler's law.) Is this relation true for all polyhedra?

Mind-Reading Cards for Bimbo

In an interesting article about the Youngs, I. Gratin-Guinness has included a section of Grace Young's reminiscences in which she describes a surprise visit.

One day, just when I was unable to receive visitors owing to Leni's arrival [a new baby daughter], a big cheery man walked in familiarly at the gate and accosted the children. When he found how things were, Dr. Young away in England and Mrs. Young invisible, he nevertheless walked right into the dining room, took Bimbo on his knee and fraternised with Auntie May showing the greatest interest in the children and winning Auntie May's heart by admiring her pet Dortchen (Janet). He told them who he was, but he might have been Gauss or Goethe for all Auntie May understood or minded. What impressed her, and what she never afterwards forgot, was his unconventional friendliness.

It was Georg Cantor, certainly the greatest of German mathematicians of that day.

. . . He remembered his visit and kept up his interest in the children. To Bimbo he sent (in 1907) some cards, carefully written with his own hand, by means of which Bimbo was immediately able to divine numbers thought of by

other people. . . . Bimbo was much interested in this game and set out to find the principle on which the cards were constructed. I am not sure if he actually succeeded in doing so; it depends simply on the binary system of numeration.[20]

A recent reissue of the Youngs' book *The Theory of Sets and Points* includes an introduction by Cecily Tanner, one of their daughters. In it she includes the letter Cantor wrote to the family when he sent the game.

I wish to give your Frankie something that will give him pleasure, as well as food for thought, and for this purpose I have inscribed eight cards with the numbers 1 to 255.

With their help he will be able to guess any number between these limits that another person thinks of. To do so he has only to find out on which of these cards the number appears; by adding up the initial numbers on the cards concerned he will obtain the number with unfailing certainty. The root of the matter, as you will at once perceive, is the unique representation of whole numbers in the dyadic system.[21]

To try the trick, cut out the strips in Figure 9-7. (These cards will work for guessing numbers from 0 through 31.) Follow the directions in Cantor's letter as follows.

1. Present strips.
2. Subject examines strips and reports those on which mystery number appears.
3. Reveal mystery number. It is the sum of the first numbers of each strip which contains it.
4. Example: Mystery number is 11. 11 appears on strips B, D, and E. First number on B is 8, on D is 2, on E is 1. Therefore mystery number is 8 + 2 + 1 = 11, which is correct!

A	B	C	D	E
				1
			2	
			3	3
		4		
		5		5
		6	6	
		7	7	7
	8			
	9			9
	10		10	
	11		11	11
	12	12		
	13	13		13
	14	14	14	
	15	15	15	15
16				
17				17
18			18	
19			19	19
20		20		
21		21		21
22		22	22	
23		23	23	23
24	24			
25	25			25
26	26		26	
27	27		27	27
28	28	28		
29	29	29		29
30	30	30	30	
31	31	31	31	31

Figure 9-7. Mind-Reading Cards

The "dyadic system" to which Cantor refers is the binary system. This number system has only two numerals, 0 and 1, and is ideally suited to electronic devices where these two states can be represented by *on* and *off*. Every number, then, can be represented by some collection of 0's and 1's. The place values parallel the base 10 system to which we are accustomed, but successive columns increase by powers of 2 instead of power of 10.

Can you extend the system to 255 as Cantor did in his present to Bimbo? What would the eight columns look like now?

Table 9-2

BINARY NUMBERS

	16	8	4	2	1
0					0
1					1
2				1	0
3				1	1
4			1	0	0
5			1	0	1
6			1	1	0
7			1	1	1
8		1	0	0	0
9		1	0	0	1
10		1	0	1	0
11		1	0	1	1
12		1	1	0	0
13		1	1	0	1
14		1	1	1	0
15		1	1	1	1
16	1	0	0	0	0
17	1	0	0	0	1
18	1	0	0	1	0
19	1	0	0	1	1
20	1	0	1	0	0
21	1	0	1	0	1
22	1	0	1	1	0
23	1	0	1	1	1
24	1	1	0	0	0
25	1	1	0	0	1
26	1	1	0	1	0
27	1	1	0	1	1
28	1	1	1	0	0
29	1	1	1	0	1
30	1	1	1	1	0
31	1	1	1	1	1

Emmy Noether   1882–1935

Sonya Kovalevskaya was a grown woman of 34 and Grace Young a 14-year-old girl when Emmy Noether was born in Germany in 1882. Like Hypatia and Maria Agnesi before her, she was the daughter of a mathematician and university professor.

Not much has been written about the life of Emmy Noether. The major available source of information is the warm, moving eulogy written by her colleague Hermann Weyl when she died unexpectedly in 1935. Emmy's work was fundamental, generating many ideas which continue to suggest research problems of the first importance. At the time of her death Einstein wrote about her in the New York Times: "In the judgment of the most competent living mathematicians, Fräulein Noether was the most significant creative mathematical genius thus far' produced since the higher education of women began."[1]

Growing Up

Emmy Noether grew up in the peaceful university town of Erlangen in southern Germany, where her father, Max Noether, was a member of the faculty. There were four children in the family; Emmy was the oldest and the only girl. Two of her brothers died young. The third, Fritz, also became a mathematician.

It is fortunate for mathematics that Emmy Noether grew up at a time that higher education for women was becoming more accessible in Germany. She probably would have lacked the drive necessary to overcome the kinds of obstacles faced by some of her predecessors.

Emmy's childhood was happy and secure. Max Noether had been professor at the University since 1875, and he was to remain there until he died in 1921. Emmy Noether's personality is said to have been a perfect reflection of the Noether household; she was warm, easy going, and happy.

While she was growing up, Emmy lived the typical life of a young woman of her class. She helped with the housework, cooked, and went to dances. She does not seem to have been an exceptional student in any way. In fact, as a young student she seemed to prefer the study of languages. After leaving secondary school she passed tests which qualified her to teach French and English. But at this time she decided to continue her education instead of teaching.

When she entered the University of Erlangen in the winter of 1900, Emmy Noether was one of only two women among a thousand students enrolled. At this time she started the serious study of mathematics which was to continue as long as she lived. In 1907 she completed her doctoral dissertation at the university. Her advisor was Paul Gordon, a well-known mathematician and an old family friend. Her later, more creative, work was very different from her work at this period with Gordon. During this time Emmy occasionally substituted for her father as a university lecturer when he was ill. (This is reminiscent of Maria Agnesi more than a century before.)

In 1916 Emmy went to Göttingen, where she was to remain until Hitler's rise forced her to leave the country in the thirties. Göttingen was then the principal center of mathematics in Germany and probably in all of Europe. The great mathematicians David Hilbert and Felix Klein were in Göttingen, welcomed her as a valued colleague. By this time Emmy had published half a dozen papers.

The Struggles for Position

Although being a woman had not seemed to hinder her development as a mathematician, finding a suitable job seemed an insuperable problem. Emmy Noether was as free as any man to devote herself to her work and students. She was not married, nor did she have children who might create emergencies. She had no husband whose career might divert her from her own. It could not be said that she was working merely for pin money and therefore needed no salary. Although none of the usual excuses used to bar women from these kinds of jobs were applicable in her case, the mere fact that she was a woman was sufficient to deny her a decent position.

Emmy Noether was unquestionably considered to be an outstanding mathematician at this time. Had she been a man she would have been considered a powerful addition to any faculty. Göttingen now gave doctoral degrees to women; jobs, however, were another matter. Hilbert tried in vain to obtain an appointment for her. Resistance was particularly high among the nonmathematicians on the philosophical faculty. And this resistance was clearly based on sex discrimination alone. Hilbert pushed as hard as he was able. At a faculty meeting he is said to have declared, "I do not see that the sex of the candidate is an argument against her admission as Privat-docent. After all, we are a university, not a bathing establishment."[2] But prejudice was too high, and he was unable to change any rules. He did, however, make it possible for her to lecture by announcing her lectures under his own name. Emmy Noether was not paid for these lectures. After 1919, regulations loosened sufficiently that she was given an unofficial associate professorship. This position carried only a title—no duties and still no salary. Later a modest salary was provided by a teaching appointment in algebra. But not until she came to the United States in 1933 did she receive a professorship at a level anywhere near worthy of her talents and reputation. Hermann Weyl was keenly aware of the injustice of Emmy's situation when he wrote:

> When I was called permanently to Göttingen in 1930, I earnestly tried to obtain from the Ministerium a better position for her, because I was ashamed to occupy such a preferred position beside her whom I knew to be my superior as a mathematician in many respects. I did not succeed. Tradition, prejudice, external considerations, weighted the balance against her scientific merits and scientific greatness, by that time denied by no one. In my Göttingen years, 1930–1933, she was without doubt the strongest center of mathematical activity there, considering both the fertility of her scientific research program and her influence upon a large circle of pupils. [3]

A Rare Woman, A Rare Mathematician

Emmy Noether was one of those rare exceptions to the early flowering of creativity in mathematicians. She did her most powerful work later in her life. That was the special tragedy of her early death. Weyl notes a paper presented in 1920 as the decisive turning point in her work. Then, at 39, she was on the path that was to mark her unique contribution to mathematics, the building up, on an axiomatic basis, of a completely general theory of ideals.

"It is here for the first time that the Emmy Noether appears whom we all know, and who changed the face of algebra by her work."[4] Her special strengths as a mathematician came from her ability to operate abstractly and directly with concepts. She had no need to move through the concrete to the abstract. With a vivid imagination, she was able to visualize remote connections . . . and thus constantly moved toward unification. She was able to abstract the simple underlying structures from their more complicated superstructures. Much of the power of her ideas is apparent in the work of her students. She had the gift of delivering a phrase which would "become a signpost to point the way for future difficult work." Above all, she originated "a new and epochmaking style of thinking in algebra."[5]

Despite her irregular university position at Göttingen, she exerted a great influence on a large circle of students. Weyl writes of the personal and intellectual closeness between Emmy Noether and her students, who were known as "the Noether

Emmy Noether with colleagues on an excursion at the 1932 International Mathematical Congress in Zurich. It was at this meeting that the power of Noether's achievements was affirmed by the mathematical community.

boys." Years later, at Bryn Mawr, she was to generate the same kind of atmosphere with her women students.

The 1932 International Mathematical Congress in Zurich finally brought her the recognition due her great achievements. Norbert Wiener described meeting her with her students on a train bound for the congress: " . . . a very warm personality and her many students flocked around her like a clutch of ducklings about a kind motherly hen . . . A summary of her work read by her at this gathering was the real triumph of the direction she represented, and she could look, not only with inner satisfaction, but now also with consciousness of full recognition, upon the mathematical path that she had traveled."[6]

Exile, Appointment, The End

In the spring of 1933 Emmy Noether, together with many of Germany's finest mathematicians and scientists, was forced to leave the country. She shared her fate with a distinguished company—Max Born, Courant, Landau, Bernays, and many others. The great university which had been Göttingen was scattered to the four winds. The move to Bryn Mawr was a happy one for Emmy Noether personally. For the first time in her life she enjoyed a normal faculty appointment. "She loved to walk. She would take her students off for a jaunt on a Saturday afternoon. On these trips she would become so absorbed in her conversation on mathematics that she would forget about the traffic and her students would need to protect her."[7] At Bryn Mawr her lectures were delivered in broken English. When bothered by some idea, she would often lapse back into German. She maintained close contact with the Institute for Advanced Studies at Princeton, which was close by, and spent time there as a visitor. Einstein and Weyl were there at that time. Her work, lectures, and research were exceptionally successful. All this made her sudden death one and one-half years later particularly sad.

Weyl contrasted Emmy Noether with another great woman mathematician, Sonya Kovalevskaya. Except in the undisputed quality of their work as mathematicians, the contrast between these two women is dramatic. Sonya Kovalevskaya was considered feminine and charming in appearance; Emmy Noether was said to be much different. In her biography of Hilbert, Constance Reid describes Emmy Noether as having a loud and disagreeable voice. "She looked like an energetic and near-sighted washerwoman. Her clothes were always baggy."[8]

There seems to be general agreement among those who knew her that Emmy Noether was loving, unassuming, and utterly unselfish. This again is in direct contrast with Kovalevskaya, who was extremely temperamental, demanding, and self-centered. Whereas Noether was neither rebellious nor Bohemian in her way of life, Kovalevskaya was both. Without that rebelliousness, Kovalevskaya probably could not have achieved what she did at the time and place that she lived. Emmy Noether was luckier: she lived later and was part of a family which supported her development. It is interesting, however, that Sonya, who lived the more rounded role as woman, was far less happy than Emmy. A creature of tension and whim she found mathematics a frenetic activity which gave her little pleasure. Emmy Noether, on the other hand, took the greatest pleasure in her work.

Emmy Noether died suddenly in 1935 from complications following routine surgery. She was then at the height of her creative powers. Weyl ended his eulogy, "She was a great mathematician, the greatest, I firmly believe, that her sex has ever produced, and a great woman."[9] A more recent paper about her life sums up the woman most beautifully: "...her femininity appeared in that gentle and subtle lyricism which lay at the heart of the far-flung but never superficial concerns which she maintained for people, for her profession, and for the interests of all mankind. She loved people, science, life, with all the warmth, all the cheerfulness, all the unselfishness, and all the tenderness of which a deeply sensitive—and feminine—soul is capable."[10]

Emmy Noether died at a relatively early age. Her age at her death was the sixteenth prime number.

The middle two digits of the year of her birth are the eighth multiple of the fifth prime number.

The fourth digit of her birth year is the first prime number.

Emmy Noether was born in __ __ __ __ and died in __ __ __ __ at the age of __ __ .

Emmy Noether's Work

Emmy Noether worked in a part of mathematics called abstract algebra. In this field the mathematician tries to discover the underlying structure of a problem by stripping away its nonessential features. In this way, a problem which may seem very difficult at first may be found to be basically the same as another that has been solved before. Once this is realized, the new problem is solved also. So mathematicians have described some basic structures to help them do this. These are called algebraic structures.

The Group

In this section we look at one of the simplest of these mathematical structures, the *group*. To show the process we are describing, we introduce several examples which have the same underlying structure.

Some Two-Element Groups

The following is a simple example of a group. Suppose we add two even numbers. The result will be an even number.

This is symbolized by writing $E + E = E$. For example, $2 + 4 = 6$ or $12 + 8 = 20$

We also know that $E + O = O$ or $O + E = O$ For example, $4 + 1 = 5$ or $3 + 8 = 11$

And last, we know that $O + O = E$ For example, $3 + 5 = 8$ or $7 + 11 = 18$

All this is summarized in Table 10-1.

179

Table 10-1

+	E	O
E	E	O
O	O	E

We say that the two-element set O (odd) and E (even) is a *group* under the operation addition.

Here is another example of a group, which is essentially the same: Here again we deal with a two-element set, $\{+, -\}$. Table 10-2 shows the multiplication table for this set. The entries in the table are the signs (+ or −) which are the result of the multiplication of two signed numbers. For example, $+2 \times -3 = -6$.

Table 10-2

×	+	−
+	+	−
−	−	+

Compare Table 10-2 with Table 10-1. Notice the similar pattern.

(Complete Table 10-3 before answering the next question.)

Table 10-3.

×	E	O
E		
O		

Table 10-3 is the $\{E,O\}$ set under multiplication instead of addition. Is the structure of Table 10-3 the same as that of Tables 10-1 and 10-2? What happens to the pattern now?

So far we have looked at two-element sets, $\{E,O\}$ or $\{+,-\}$. Now we look at a group made up of a three-element set. Divide all integers into three sets the following way. Any integer divided by 3 will have a remainder of either 0, 1, or 2. This *set of remainders* forms the three-element set $\{0,1,2\}$.

To see how this works, consider 7. 7≅1 since 7÷3 = 2 remainder 1 and it is the remainder we define as belonging to our set. (The symbol ≅ means "equivalent to"). This is the same idea as mod(3), discussed in Chapter 5.

For our purposes, then, 4, 7, 10, 13, . . . are the same. They are all equivalent to 1 since all of them have 1 as a remainder when they are divided by 3. Similarly, 3, 6, 9, 12, 15, . . . are all equivalent to 0, since they all have *no* remainder when divided by 3. Also, 5, 8, 11, 14, . . . are all equivalent to 2, since each of these numbers has remainder 2 when divided by 3. You should be able to see that every integer can be assigned to one of these three sets..

What happens when 0, 1, or 2 are added, two at a time, in all possible combinations? Complete Table 10-4. Notice that all the entries in Table 10-4 will be either 0, 1, or 2.

Table 10-4.

⊕	0	1	2
0			
1			
2			

A Six-Element Group

Now let's consider the set of numbers 0, 1, 2, 3, 4, 5. This is the set of remainders when any integer is divided by 6. As before, we can think of this set as positions on a clock. In such a model, the operation ⊕ would mean clockwise motion around the face of the clock. Notice that this is a *finite* set. No matter how many steps we take around the clock, the landing position will always be 0, 1, 2, 3, 4, or 5. Such a model looks like Figure 10-1.

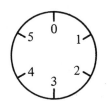

Figure 10-1.

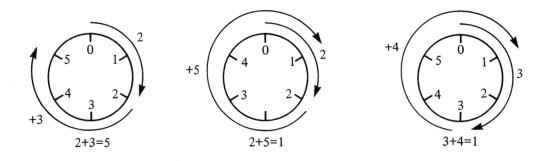

Fill in Table 10-5.

Table 10-5.

$\oplus$	0	1	2	3	4	5
0						
1						
2						
3						
4						
5						

Six-Element Permutation Groups

The next three examples are essentially the same. Although they look different, they have the same underlying structure. Mathematicians would call them *isomorphic*: *iso* means "same", *morphic* means "body" or "structure." Differences among these three, and the previous example, should also be clear. The sets we will be describing are made up of *transformations* rather than numbers.

Example 1. Arrange *A, B,* and *C* in all possible ways. There will be six ways. (Each way, or arrangement, is what is meant by a transformation.) These six ways include the identity, where the positions of the letters are unchanged.

We list these arrangements (or transformations or permutations) as follows.

$$
\begin{array}{cccccc}
\text{A B C} & \text{A B C} & \text{A B C} & \text{A B C} & \text{A B C} & \text{A B C} \\
\downarrow\downarrow\downarrow & \downarrow\downarrow\downarrow & \downarrow\downarrow\downarrow & \downarrow\downarrow\downarrow & \downarrow\downarrow\downarrow & \downarrow\downarrow\downarrow \\
A\ B\ C & C\ A\ B & B\ C\ A & A\ C\ B & C\ B\ A & B\ A\ C \\
\end{array}
$$

Call them I J K L M N

These, then, are the elements of our set $\{I, J, K, L, M, N\}$.

Next we define a new kind of operation, *, different from +, −, ×, or ÷, which tells us how to combine elements of this set. $A * B$ means 'do A, then do B'. Here's how * works.

Example: $K*J=?$ Transformation K is $\begin{pmatrix} A & B & C \\ \downarrow & \downarrow & \downarrow \\ B & C & A \end{pmatrix}$

                        Transformation J is $\begin{pmatrix} A & B & C \\ \downarrow & \downarrow & \downarrow \\ C & A & B \end{pmatrix}$

     $K*J=I$ because

$$
K*J = \begin{pmatrix} A & B & C \\ \downarrow & \downarrow & \downarrow \\ B & C & A \end{pmatrix} * \begin{pmatrix} A & B & C \\ \downarrow & \downarrow & \downarrow \\ C & A & B \end{pmatrix} = \begin{pmatrix} A & B & C \\ \downarrow & \downarrow & \downarrow \\ B & C & A \\ \downarrow & \downarrow & \downarrow \\ A & B & C \end{pmatrix} = \begin{pmatrix} A & B & C \\ \downarrow & \downarrow & \downarrow \\ A & B & C \end{pmatrix} = I
$$

Another example: $L*M=?$ $L = \begin{pmatrix} A & B & C \\ \downarrow & \downarrow & \downarrow \\ A & C & B \end{pmatrix}$ $M = \begin{pmatrix} A & B & C \\ \downarrow & \downarrow & \downarrow \\ C & B & A \end{pmatrix}$

$$
L*M = \begin{pmatrix} A & B & C \\ \downarrow & \downarrow & \downarrow \\ A & C & B \end{pmatrix} * \begin{pmatrix} A & B & C \\ \downarrow & \downarrow & \downarrow \\ C & B & A \end{pmatrix} = \begin{pmatrix} A & B & C \\ \downarrow & \downarrow & \downarrow \\ A & C & B \\ \downarrow & \downarrow & \downarrow \\ C & A & B \end{pmatrix} = \begin{pmatrix} A & B & C \\ \downarrow & \downarrow & \downarrow \\ C & A & B \end{pmatrix} = J
$$

Therefore we say, $L*M=J$. Now complete Table 10-6 showing the way all the elements in this set combine. Notice that every *2* elements combine to form some element within the set.

Table 10-6.

*	I	J	K	L	M	N
I			K			
J						
K		I				
L				I		
M	M					
N						

The Identity Element. I is the identity element for this set. (The identity element is the 'no transformation' element.

The Inverse Element. K*J=I, so we say *K* is the inverse of *J*; and *J* is the inverse of *K*. Every element in Table 10-6 has an inverse. The inverse of every element is another element, which combines with it, to form the identity.

An example from arithmetic:

Let * be +.
Let *J* be 5.
Since *I* is 0 (0 is the identity in arithmetic when * is +),
K would be ⁻5, since 5 + ⁻5 = 0.

Another example from arithmetic:

Let * be ✕.
Now *I* is 1 (since 1 is the identity under multiplication).
Then if *J* is 5,
K must be 1/5 since *J*K=I* translates to 5✕(1/5)=1.

Complete Figure 10-1 below. (All the information needed is in Table 10-6.)

$$I* \underline{\hspace{1cm}} =I; \qquad J* \underline{\hspace{1cm}} =I; \qquad K* \underline{\hspace{1cm}} =I;$$

$$L* \underline{\hspace{1cm}} =I; \qquad M* \underline{\hspace{1cm}} =I; \qquad N* \underline{\hspace{1cm}} =I.$$

Figure 10-1.

Example 2: Permutation Dominoes. The permutation dominoes are another representation of the same transformations as letters *A, B, C* in example 1. Can you see why?

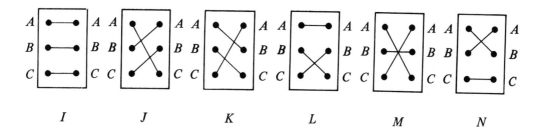

$$I \qquad J \qquad K \qquad L \qquad M \qquad N$$

Call this set of transformations $\{I, J, K, L, M, N\}$. Note how I, J, K, L, M, N in this example relates to example 1.

We combine elements of this set using the * operation. For example, $K*J=I$ because

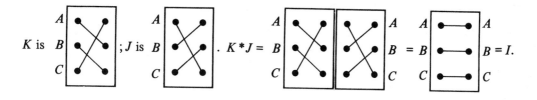

Since A goes through B back to A, B goes through C back to B, and C goes through A back to C, we say $K*J=I$.

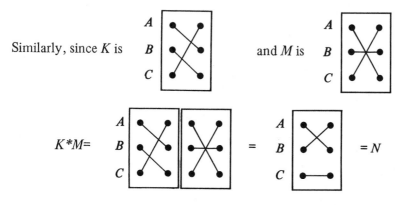

Since A goes through A to B, B goes through C to A, and C goes through A to C. Complete Table 10-7 on p. 186.

If you need help visualizing the result of *, cut out the dominoes shown in Figure 10-2 and push pairs together to see how they combine. Compare the results of Table 10-7 with Table 10-6.

Table 10-7.

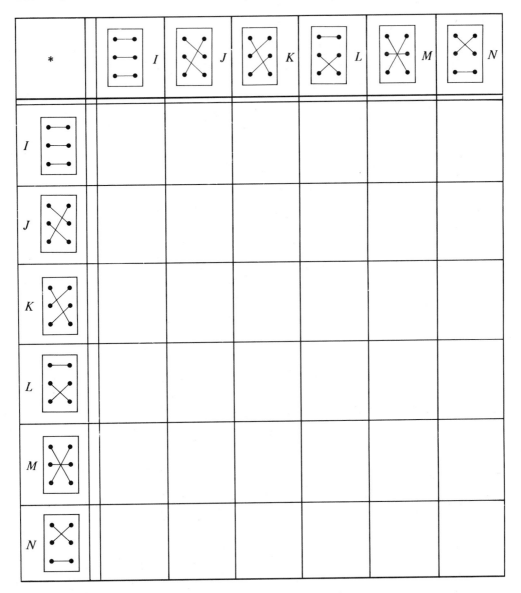

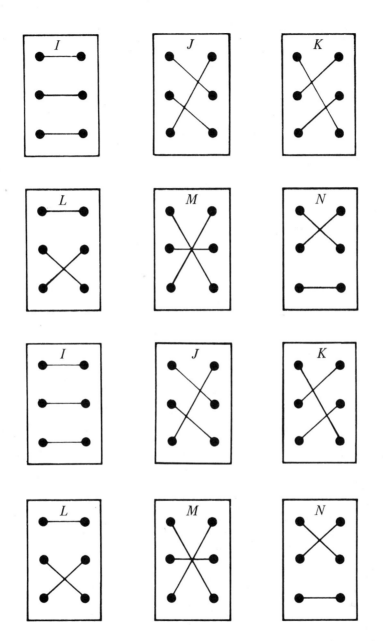

Figure 10-2.

Check that all the resulting combinations are indeed within the original set. (This is the group property called *closure*. All groups must have this property.)

Check that the operation is associative, that is, $(J*M)*L=J*(M*L)$. (All groups must also have this property.)

Make sure you know which element is the *identity element*. (All groups must have this special element as a member of the set.)

Draw and name the *inverse* for each element below.

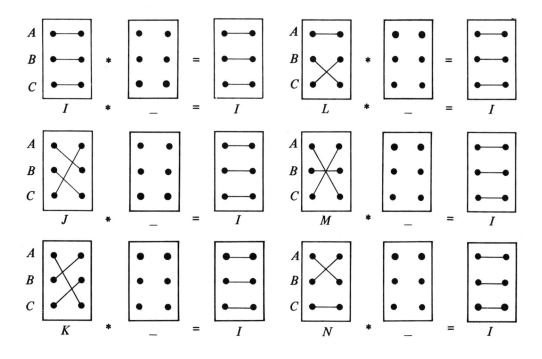

Is this a commutative group?

That is, is ... ?

Example 3. Consider the rotations and flips of an equilateral triangle whose vertices are labeled *A, B,* and C. Note that *I, J* and *K* are transformations which describe rotations of the triangle, while *L, M,* and *N* are transformations which describe flips; for example, is flipped around line *AD*; vertex *A* is a pivot and remains constant, while *C* and *B* are exchanged. In this way goes to On the dominoes we saw this same transformation in *L,* where the top line was unchanged and B and C were crossed.

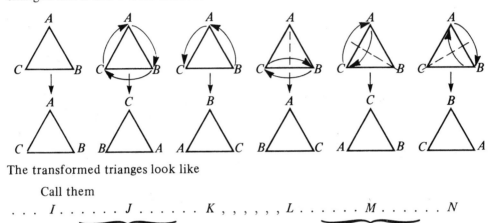

The transformed trianges look like

Call them

. . . *I* . . . . . . *J* . . . . . . *K* , , , , , , *L* . . . . *M* . . . . . *N*

Cyclic rotations   Flips

Again we define operation * so that A*B means "do transformation A, then do transformation B."

Complete Table 10-7. If necessary, cut and label a triangle and actually carry out the transformations. Can you answer the same kinds of questions for this group as were asked for the permutation dominoes group? Since these groups are isomorphic and have the same structure, the answers should be the same, though they may appear different.

Check that this set, with * as its operation, does indeed have the structure we call a *group*. (Check Appendix 9 for the formal group properties.)

Table 10-7.

*	$\begin{array}{c}ABC\\\downarrow\downarrow\downarrow\\ABC\end{array}$ I	$\begin{array}{c}ABC\\\downarrow\downarrow\downarrow\\BCA\end{array}$ J	$\begin{array}{c}ABC\\\downarrow\downarrow\downarrow\\CAB\end{array}$ K	$\begin{array}{c}ABC\\\downarrow\downarrow\downarrow\\ACB\end{array}$ L	$\begin{array}{c}ABC\\\downarrow\downarrow\downarrow\\CBA\end{array}$ M	$\begin{array}{c}ABC\\\downarrow\downarrow\downarrow\\BAC\end{array}$ N
I						
J						
K						
L						
M						
N						

Extensions

1.   Instead of set $\{0, 1, 2, 3, 4, 5\}$, consider set $\{0, 1, 2, 3, 4, 5, 6, 7\}$. Make sure you remember what the operation $\oplus$ means. Fill in a table showing that this set forms a group under the operation $\oplus$.

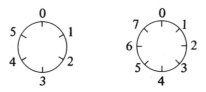

2.   Instead of the rotations and flips of an equilateral triangle (Example 3 above) look at the rotations and flips of the following figure. Can you complete the labeling of the figures below, showing them after their various transformations?

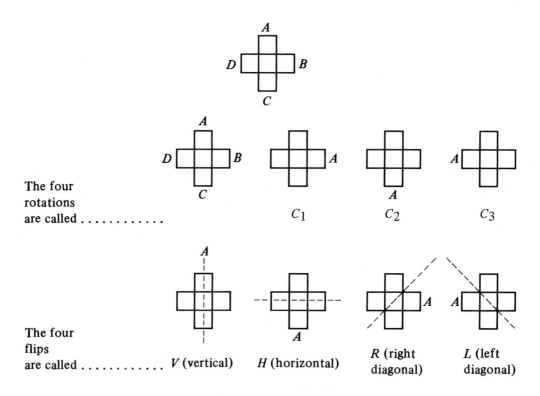

The four rotations are called . . . .

The four flips are called . . . .   V (vertical)   H (horizontal)   R (right diagonal)   L (left diagonal)

The flips are around the horizontal axis (through DB), the vertical axis (through AC), the right diagonal, and the left diagonal. For simplicity let us list these transformations by letters only.

Then $I =$
$$
\begin{array}{cccc}
A & B & C & D \\
\downarrow & \downarrow & \downarrow & \downarrow \\
A & B & C & D
\end{array}
$$
$C1 =$
$$
\begin{array}{cccc}
A & B & C & D \\
\downarrow & \downarrow & \downarrow & \downarrow \\
B & C & D & A
\end{array}
$$
$C2 =$
$$
\begin{array}{cccc}
A & B & C & D \\
\downarrow & \downarrow & \downarrow & \downarrow \\
C & D & A & B
\end{array}
$$
$C3 =$
$$
\begin{array}{cccc}
A & B & C & D \\
\downarrow & \downarrow & \downarrow & \downarrow \\
D & A & B & C
\end{array}
$$

I, C1, C2, and C3 are the 4 cyclic transformations.

$V =$
$$
\begin{array}{cccc}
A & B & C & D \\
\downarrow & \downarrow & \downarrow & \downarrow \\
A & D & C & B
\end{array}
$$
$H =$
$$
\begin{array}{cccc}
A & B & C & D \\
\downarrow & \downarrow & \downarrow & \downarrow \\
C & B & A & D
\end{array}
$$
$R =$
$$
\begin{array}{cccc}
A & B & C & D \\
\downarrow & \downarrow & \downarrow & \downarrow \\
B & A & D & C
\end{array}
$$
$L =$
$$
\begin{array}{cccc}
A & B & C & D \\
\downarrow & \downarrow & \downarrow & \downarrow \\
D & C & B & A
\end{array}
$$

(vertical flip   (horizontal flip   (right diagonal   (left diagonal
around AC)   around DB)   flip)   flip)

Use either form to complete the chart and establish the group properties. Can you design a set of permutation dominoes which will show this same structure?

The total number of permutations of three letters is $3 \times 2 \times 1 = 6$. Our earlier example included all of these. The total number of permutations of four letters is $4 \times 3 \times 2 \times 1 = 24$. So why do only eight permutations appear in this model?

A Puzzle

Here is a puzzle that may be interesting. What you have learned about groups should help you think about how it works. Anne suggests a "fair" and amusing way to decide whether she, Matt, or Joe will do the dinner dishes that evening.

First she draws three vertical lines on a sheet of paper, labeling each line at the top with one of the three initials (*Anne*, *Matt*, *Joe*). See Figure 10-3. Then she folds the paper horizontally so the initials cannot be seen.

Matt marks an X at the bottom of any one of the three vertical lines. Then he arbitrarily draws some horizontal lines connecting the vertical lines; any number of lines may connect any verticals. Note, however, that these horizontal lines only connect *any two* vertical lines. For example, line *CD* does not cross the second vertical line. Instead it forms a bridge ($\cap$) crossing *over* it, connecting the first and third verticals.

Joe adds a few more horizontal lines . . . and the puzzle is ready. (The number of lines added make no difference to how well the puzzle works.)

When as many horizontal lines as desired have been added, the paper is unfolded; the initials are now visible again.

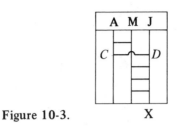

Figure 10-3.

Each player takes a turn tracing a path through the figure, starting down the vertical line headed by his or her initial.

To trace a proper path, follow a vertical line until it intersects a horizontal line. At that point continue the path along the horizontal to the vertical with which it intersects; then continue vertically down until the next horizontal, and so on until the bottom.

The player whose path ends on the X is the loser!

What is interesting to note here is that no matter where, or how many horizontal lines have been drawn on the figure or where they appear, each path traced will always end at a *different* position.

Figure 10-4 shows an example.

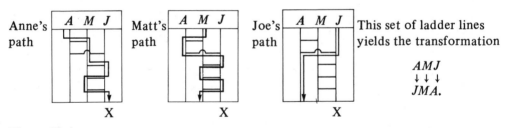

Figure 10-4.

Try a new array of your own. Can you dig out the group structure? Hint: Consider a simpler case first, one with only one or two horizontal lines.

The Problem and Some Exciting Solutions

For some reason which is not yet clear, the role of mathematician seems to have been defined long ago as a male one. As a result, mathematically gifted women have had to deal with many special problems before they have been able to develop and enjoy their talents. For a woman, talent alone would probably not have been a sufficient criterion for success in mathematics. Other qualities, such as the drive and determination to ignore role stereotypes, would have been necessary as well. The women in this book are among the few we know who have managed to do so successfully in the past. Therefore it may be useful to review some of the special advantages and problems which were part of their histories.

Advantages and Disadvantages

The women we have been writing about enjoyed certain advantages which most women of their times did not. All of them were from either academic or wealthy, upper-class families. Some came from both backgrounds. The Marquise Du Châtelet and Countess Lovelace were from the French and English aristocracy, and so could command the services of outstanding mathematicians as teachers. Hypatia, Agnesi, and Noether were daughters of mathematicians. Growing up in homes where mathematics was known and appreciated, their talents were easily recognized, developed, and encouraged. At a time when public libraries did not exist, access to books was a crucial factor—and the families of some of these women had fine private libraries. Mary Somerville writes about how happy she was when, at 33, she finally had the money and independence to buy the books she needed to continue to study.

Although these women enjoyed certain advantages, they shared, with all women, many disadvantages.

The Obstacle of Education

With few exceptions, education for girls and women was until very recently either non-existent or was restricted to the "homely" arts. Even where women received the equivalent of a secondary school education, colleges—and until more recently, graduate schools—were closed to them. This was true even for the most gifted or well-qualified women.

At the time Sonya Kovalevskaya was young, all Russian universities were closed to women. One of the few ways for a young Russian woman to continue her education was to marry in order to be free to study abroad. This, in fact, is what Sonya Kovalevskaya and many of her young friends did. Even abroad, she was not permitted to attend lectures at the University of Berlin when she needed to continue her studies there. It was only through the kindness of Weierstrass, who worked with her privately, that Sonya Kovalevskaya was able to complete her training.

Sophie Germain before her had been unable to attend the Ecole Polytechnic since it also was closed to women. Her determination and audacity were important factors in making possible her continued education. These qualities, having nothing to do with her talents as a mathematician, were crucial to her mathematical development. Believing that only men could command serious attention, Sophie submitted a paper under a male pseudonym to the famous French mathematician Laplace. It was Laplace's response and subsequent support which opened to her the world of mathematics of her time.

Grace Chisholm, living at the beginning of the twentieth century, was still breaking new ground at each step of her education, first getting to Cambridge despite her family's plans for her, then having to leave England to do graduate work. Not until a generation later were her daughters able to remain in England for graduate work. Even in Emmy Noether's time, with higher education finally becoming more accessible to women, few women were prepared to take advantage of the opportunities as they arose. Emmy Noether entered the University of Erlangen in 1900 as one of only two women among a thousand students.

Parents, Teachers, and Role Stereotypes

Several of the stories in this book contain references to deep prejudice against women studying "brainy" subjects such as mathematics. This prejudice seems rooted in the feeling that women were made for childbearing, and that "brain work" would in some way conflict with this primary biological function. Breakdown, both mental and physical, was feared, were women to deny their biological destiny. Sophie Germain's parents, genuinely worried, went to great lengths to obstruct her studies.

Even if parents did not create problems, teachers sometimes did. Augustus DeMorgan's letter to Lady Byron, Ada's mother, is an example of the effect of such fears. Because he cared about Ada and feared that such study might be physically harmful, DeMorgan felt obliged to be frugal with his encouragement as she progressed.

And finally, even with supportive parents and teachers, the traditional female roles of wife, mother, and homemaker made study at advanced levels difficult. Husbands could cause problems. Mary Somerville probably would not have been able to achieve what she did except for the early death of her first husband, a man strongly opposed to serious study for women. In her second marriage she was fortunate to find a husband both sympathetic and supportive. Many of the women mathematicians included here—Hypatia, Agnesi, Germain, and Noether—were never married. Sonya Kovalevskaya was married, but she lived with her husband only briefly. Du Châtelet, Somerville, and Lovelace were of sufficiently high social class to have servants, so although married they were relatively free to work. Grace Young raised her children with the help of maiden aunts, so she too was able to continue to be productive, though married and the mother of a large family.

Women often saw themselves in terms of the stereotypes of the times in which they lived. We see examples of this even among the women in this book. Mary Somerville, presented with the work of a male colleague who had extended some work of hers in a way she had not herself thought of, was not surprised. "Of course," she wrote, "God has not given such gifts for original genius to women."[1] When Ada Lovelace was particularly excited about some work she had done, she wrote "I am very much satisfied with this first child of mine. He is an uncommonly fine baby, and will grow to be a man of the first magnitude and power."[2] Her work was not just her child, it was her male child.

The Professional Obstacles

Even when able to obtain sufficient education to move to the front of their professions. Women found themselves faced with problems and barriers because they were unique women. In some ways these have proved the most stubborn obstacles. Kovalevskaya fought and struggled for her position at every stage of her career. Without a suitable ally, Mittag-Leffler, and a new liberal university in Sweden, her career would probably have been blocked. She was never able to get a decent job in her own country, Russia.

Professional employment for women in Germany was difficult even into the twentieth century. Emmy Noether never received a position in her own country that matched her reputation in the mathematical community.

Women have often had trouble getting credit for their work. A letter to Grace Young from her husband William is an amazing example of this problem, even between people as close as husband and wife. *She*, he writes, has the babies. *He*—for the time being—will take the credit for their work together.

Burial by History

It is true the list of obstacles women have had to face in the past is impressive, and it is not surprising that we have not heard of more women who overcame them. But a more careful look at history may show that far more women than we realize *did* manage to surmount all the obstacles and make significant contributions. As people begin to do historical research in new areas, surprises emerge. The contributions of women to mathematics may be such an area. We know, for example, that different historians notice, select, and record different events. We also know that for long periods it was considered improper for women to sign their own work. This was true in literature and art as well as in mathematics. Ada Lovelace's paper was signed A.A.L. Readers without special information would have had no way of knowing that the work was done by a woman. Few people know of the *Ladies' Diary*, a magazine published in England from the beginning of the eighteenth century to the mid-nineteenth century. This magazine intended, "to employ Some Spare Hours of the Fair-Sex in a Study Innocent, Useful, and Diverting."[3] was devoted almost entirely to problems and puzzles in mathematics. The *Ladies' Diary* contained many contributions by women. That such a magazine existed at that time is a surprise, yet demonstrates an early interest in mathematics by women, one sufficient to support a magazine similar in function to today's *Scientific American*.

The Picture Today

What about women and mathematics today? What is happening to some of the barriers?

In the United States elementary and secondary education is equally available to men and women. Admission to universities is also accessible to qualified women. Sex discrimination is probably not a problem at this stage. Long before the college years, however, subtle social pressures cause young women to withdraw from mathematics at the secondary school level in far greater numbers than boys of equal ability. This happens even though studies show no significant differences in the way boys and girls rate their preference for mathematics compared with other subjects. In secondary school, mathematics begins to become more difficult for both boys and girls. Boys, under pressure to have careers, seem more aware of the importance of mathematics— sociologist Lucy Sells has called it a "critical filter." Only the most stereotypically female areas do not require mathematics as a prerequisite. So boys are pressed to continue to study mathematics, whereas girls with equal mental endowment are allowed, often *encouraged*, to stop. Experience, however, is showing that a relatively small amount of counseling or role modeling for girls can cause significant changes in these patterns.

Admission to graduate schools in the United States is probably now nondiscriminatory to qualified women. Except for a brief period in the twenties and early thirties, however, this has not been the case until very recently. It is interesting to consider what happened to the women who received graduate degrees in those decades. Perhaps we may learn something useful for young women being educated now. Have women with PhD's had access to jobs of the same quality as male colleagues of equivalent ability? Have women been fully included in the interaction and sharing of ideas which is so important to the generation of new research?

Access to jobs at first-rate universities is important for women who want to do research, since these are the places where fundamental research is usually done. Such positions provide opportunities for interaction with colleagues who are actively involved in research. This kind of interaction stimulates ideas and encourages productive research.

Even a superficial look shows that women who have been awarded graduate degrees have not gotten jobs at the best universities. This fact is not surprising in relation to the earlier period. That it is still the case today, five years after the introduction of affirmative action programs, is much more difficult to believe. Yet the numbers are available, shocking and depressing.

Because, in the words of one woman mathematician, "In the short run, the state of the art is transmitted orally." Women excluded from this kind of interaction cannot hope to develop professionally at the same rate as their male colleagues.

Social mores in general have created serious employment problems for women. Where positions have been available to a married couple in different locations, it has been usual for the woman to follow her husband, often to the detriment of her own career. The rule against nepotism, stating that only one person in a family may be employed by an institution, is another employment practice that has been widely used against women. Where a couple has had children, the woman has traditionally taken prime responsibility for their care. Even when child care has been provided, women have generally found themselves burdened in a way not usually shared by men. Undoubtedly there are exceptions here. However, social attitudes do not dictate that the husband must share child care. Such factors doubtless set limits on the professional achievement of many women, certainly when such achievement is measured against male productivity. These effects may be seen most clearly in the countries of eastern Europe. There, although women have had full economic equality for many years, men continue to hold the most prominent professional positions. In those societies, however, the roles of women in relation to the family have remained completely traditional. So, in effect, women do a double job. They are free to work an equal day with men, but once home they are expected to care for their families with little or no help from men.

The Promise Now

The situation just now is exciting. For the second time in less than a hundred years we are seeing the emergence of a woman's movement. Again women are acting to extend the choices available to them.

The women's movement at the beginning of the twentieth century failed in many important ways. After a struggle women succeeded in winning the vote—only to find that so many compromises had been made along the way that the movement lacked the strength to use the vote effectively. Today, women are again working together to open more doors. The doors they need to open now are more resistant. To make progress now, social mores must be challenged as well as affirmative action programs implemented.

Several positive things happening in mathematics today are already beginning to make a difference. In January 1971, a group of women met spontaneously at the Atlantic City meeting of the American Mathematical Society (AMS) to talk about ways to deal with their special problems and concerns as women mathematicians. As a result of this meeting, a mathematician and professor from American University, Mary Gray, decided to organize an ongoing group to deal with such issues. In May 1971, Mary Gray distributed the first issue of a newsletter she had written, and AWM (American Women in Mathematics) was on its way!

Lenore Blum, president of AWM in 1975 and 1976, tells of her first involvement with the group. Her initial reaction was skepticism. As a promising young mathematician, she found herself unsympathetic to the idea of being identified as a *woman* mathematician, and doubtful of the value of women getting together in this way. But when she was attending an early meeting of AWM she noticed something which caused her to change her mind. Among the 50 or 60 people at that meeting in Las Vegas in 1972, half were men and many were chairmen of mathematics departments at universities. Affirmative action programs were just then being pressed on universities by the federal government, and these people were curious to learn something about what those programs would bring. The meeting began with some brief remarks by Mary Gray, and then was opened to questions from the floor. It was at this point that Lenore realized that no women were speaking; only the men were asking questions. In fact, some women, attending with men, were asking questions through the men. Watching this from the back of the room, Lenore suddenly found herself standing and saying, "I don't see a single woman making any comments here or talking. The situation looks like it is very hard for women to talk here. I think what we ought to do is call a meeting of women only." Mary Gray said she couldn't sanction that as an AWM meeting, but if Lenore Blum wanted to do it on her own that would be perfectly all right and Mary Gray would come.[4]

And so posters were improvised and the meeting was announced for the following afternoon. It was to be a meeting for women only. About 100 women showed up—a surprisingly large turnout. One of the earliest functions of this group, as of those like it in other professional societies, was to serve as a consciousness-raising body. Women needed first to share their experiences in order to discover their strengths. Then they could begin to sort out their problems, to distinguish those which were personal from the far greater number caused by roles given women in modern society.

AWM is now having a decided impact within the mathematical community. During the first five years of its existence it has grown to an organization of more than 1200 members. About 20 percent of its members are men. The organization has

Lenore Blum talking to students after her calculus class at Mills College.

notably wide support among women mathematicians. Essentially all the academic and research women in mathematics belong.

Presently, the membership of AWM reflects its origin, the research-oriented American Mathematical Society. AWM has effected many significant changes within the AMS itself. For the first time women are serving on the council or governing body of the AMS. Mary Gray was recently elected as the first woman vice-president of AMS. The numbers of women giving major talks and chairing and organizing sessions at AMS meetings has increased enormously. Also, for the first time, women are receiving important research fellowships. In short women are becoming part of the mainstream of mathematical research.

A major objective of AWM is now to broaden the organization to include a wider range of people than research mathematicians alone—mathematics educators and mathematicians in industry and government at all levels—in fact to include all women (and of course men too) who are in careers that use mathematics in any important way and who are concerned with problems that relate to women in mathematics.

One of the major activities of AWM is the distribution of a newsletter eight times a year. Looking through these, one finds articles dealing with many of the problems that concern women mathematicians. Since a fundamental ongoing concern is the search for decent jobs, each newsletter contains listings of job openings. Studies initiated by AWM spotlight the de facto discrimination in employment which becomes obvious when one looks at the numbers. So AWM is actively supporting affirmative action and trying to focus on specific cases of discrimination. The newsletter also discusses meetings and current research being done by women.

Some of the most interesting material in the newsletter involves women wrestling with the social implications of being professional women. One thread running through the newsletters is the "two-city problem." These are case histories of couples who are dealing with the problems of holding jobs in different cities. Social values have now been shaken enough so it is no longer assumed that woman must follow man when job offers in different cities arise. Of course this problem is not related to women working in mathematics alone; it concerns any couple if both partners are developing major careers. Other problems relating to couples are being considered. Whose career should have precedence? Should a couple have children? If they do have children, how shall they deal with them? Feminists feel that women will never be as free as men until men share equal responsibility for child care.

Research now under way is trying to pinpoint social factors that prevent women from developing skills in such areas as science and mathematics. Indications that applying very little pressure at critical stages results in significant changes in current patterns makes such research exciting. We see, for example, the importance of proper counseling. Counseled to do so, women will take an examination and often qualify for an honors math course, whereas before, without counseling, would not have done so and would be ineligible by default.

Colleges are experimenting with precalculus courses to give students a second chance to move into the math sequences required for many careers. Such second chances may be particularly important to young women who have been inadequately counseled in school, or who now realize that, for them, being simply wife and mother is insufficient. Role models for young people in general and for women in particular are also important. To provide these, career days are being developed during which girls meet women whose professions require mathematical skills.

The Future

As we saw earlier, Einstein wrote that Emmy Noether was "the most significant creative mathematical genius thus far produced since the higher education of women began."[5] Since this higher education essentially began in her own generation, the payoff of this "equal education" seems to have been swift and strong. The future seems promising, as the problems which are present and real are met and solved.

To answer the question, "How come there are so few great women mathematicians?" we suggest that as the numbers of women working at the frontiers of mathematics increase, so surely will the numbers of gifted women mathematicians increase.

Women mathematicians are making fundamental contributions to contemporary mathematics. Among them are many brilliant, interesting, vital women who find their work a fulfilling part of their lives.

Activity: A Hidden Mathematicians Puzzle

The first activity in this book was a hidden mathematicians puzzle. It contained the names of twenty-nine mathematicians, among them the nine women included in this book. This last activity is another hidden mathematicians puzzle. It contains the last names of contemporary women mathematicians. Since "contemporary women mathematicians" is a large set, we placed the following boundaries on our choices. First, all the women in the puzzle are members of AWM. Many are women who have been actively involved in AWM, and whose names appear frequently as contributors to the newsletter. Also included are a few personal friends and people whose work we know and particularly admire, such as Edna Kramer. Finally, since juggling names in this kind of puzzle is tricky, an AWM woman mathematician with a three- or four-letter name enjoyed a much greater probability of being selected than one with a longer name. This selection is in no way a judgment on the level of mathematical contribution of any woman who has been included or excluded here.

The names included in the puzzle lie along horizontal, vertical, or diagonal lines. Complete columns A and B in Table 11-1. Write the number pair (row and column) which locates the first letter of each name in column A. Write the number pair which locates the second letter of the name, in column B.

Can you tell, by looking at the number pairs, how the names are directed in the puzzle? For example, *KOPELL* starts at (2,4) and ends at (2,9). The row is the same, in both cases. Since *K* starts in column 4 and *L* is in column 9, *KOPELL* must appear horizontally in row 2, reading left to right from column 4 to column 9.

Hidden Mathematicians Puzzle—Contemporary Women

	1	2	3	4	5	6	7	8	9	10	11	12	13	14	15
1	R	A	E	B	R	O	M	A	W	H	E	E	L	E	R
2	N	E	L	K	O	P	E	L	L	O	R	E	L	D	E
3	A	U	F	R	E	P	P	O	H	A	A	K	A	N	O
4	M	O	R	A	W	E	T	Z	Y	B	I	R	M	A	N
5	R	I	E	M	H	T	N	K	E	N	E	E	R	G	E
6	O	A	H	E	E	C	S	I	S	R	A	O	O	E	U
7	O	M	A	R	B	F	S	O	U	L	T	U	B	I	H
8	B	T	R	Y	O	T	M	D	E	H	G	R	I	W	L
9	U	A	M	S	E	I	I	E	S	O	R	O	N	I	E
10	B	Y	O	I	L	N	T	C	I	E	A	O	S	A	N
11	A	L	N	N	E	R	H	M	S	P	Y	T	O	M	B
12	R	O	O	S	A	I	J	E	A	R	O	A	N	R	E
13	O	R	E	V	L	O	K	I	T	N	A	R	M	O	C
14	W	A	L	D	A	Y	E	R	E	S	T	R	O	M	K

Find the names of the women mathematicians hidden in this puzzle. These names may be found along horizontal, vertical, or diagonal paths of squares.

Table 11-1

Contemporary Women Mathematicians			Their Fields
	A	B	
Barrett, Lida	——	——	Topology; applied mathematics
Birman, Joan	——	——	Algebra; topology
Blum, Lenore	——	——	Logic and foundations; algebra and theory of numbers; applied mathematics
Boorman, Evelyn	——	——	Algebra; theory of numbers
Bram, Leila	——	——	Analytic number theory
Day, Jane	——	——	Algebra and theory of numbers; topology; Topological semigroups
Elkins, Judith	——	——	Analysis; complex variables; approximation theory
Gray, Mary	——	——	Algebra and theory of numbers
Green, Judy	——	——	Logic and foundations
Harmon, Adelaide	——	——	Mathematics education
Hopper, Grace	——	——	Computer science
Keen, Linda	——	——	Analysis
Kopell, Nancy	——	——	Applied math; analysis
Kramer, Edna	——	——	Algebra and theory of numbers; analysis; applied math; statistics and probability
Mayes, Vivienne	——	——	Algebra and theory of numbers
Milnor, Tilla	——	——	Geometry
Morawetz, Cathleen	——	——	Applied math
Osofsky, Barbara	——	——	Algebra and theory of numbers; Logic and foundations
Resek, Diane	——	——	Logic and foundations
Robinson, Julia	——	——	Number theoretical decision problems; recursive functions
Roitman, Judith	——	——	Logic and foundations; set theory; topology
Rothschild, Linda	——	——	Analysis; geometry
Rudin, Mary Ellen	——	——	Topology
Schafer, Alice	——	——	Algebra and theory of numbers; geometry
Smith, Martha	——	——	Algebra and theory of numbers
Stehney, Ann	——	——	Geometry
Stein, Marjorie	——	——	Linear systems; discrete math
Stone, Dorothy M.	——	——	Analysis
Taylor, Jean	——	——	Analysis; geometry
Uhlenbeck, Karen	——	——	Infinite dimensional differential topology; analysis
Wheeler, Mary	——	——	Applied math; analysis; numerical analysis
Wiegand, Sylvia	——	——	Abstract algebra

Appendix 1
Venn Diagrams

A Venn diagram pictures sets and the relationships between them. In this model, a closed curve divides the plane into two regions, inside and outside.

When membership in a set is well defined, all elements which belong to the set are represented *inside* the closed curve, usually a circle or ellipse. All elements which do not belong to the set are represented outside.

Intersecting curves represent more complex relationships between sets. Overlapping regions indicate common attributes.

For example: if set A = the first nine multiples of 2

$$= \{2, 4, 6, 8, 10, 12, 14, 16, 18\}$$

and set B = the first six multiples of 3

$$= \{3, 6, 9, 12, 15, 18\}$$

then the Venn diagram representing these sets would look like Figure A-1.

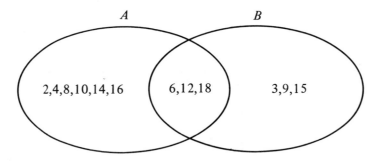

Figure A-1.

Notice that 2, 4, 8, 10, 14, 16 are in A and not in B;
3, 9, 15 are in B and not in A; and 6, 12, and 18 are in both A and B.

Appendix 2
Key Geometric Concepts

If you are uncertain of the meanings of the geometric concepts used in this book, use these definitions.

circle: The set of all points in the plane which are equally distant from a single point.

radius: (of a circle) A line segment which connects the center of a circle to any point on its circumference.

concentric: (circles) A set of circles that share a common center.

polygon: A simple closed figure formed by the union of line segments.

triangle: A polygon formed by three line segments.

square: A polygon formed by four line segments.

pentagon: A polygon formed by five line segments.

hexagon: A polygon formed by six line segments.

heptagon: A polygon formed by seven line segments.

octagon: A polygon formed by eight line segments.

nonagon: A polygon formed by nine line segments.

inscribe: A polygon is inscribed in a circle when all its corners (vertices) touch the circle.

circumscribe: A circle circumscribes a polygon when the polygon is inscribed in the circle.

A polygon circumscribes a circle when all its edges are tangent to the circle, (touch it at one point).

Appendix 3
Analytic Geometry

This section will answer the following questions:

What is a *coordinate system* in the plane?

What is a *number pair*?

What is an *ordered pair*?

How are number pairs represented in the plane? How do we graph number pairs?

Every point in the plane may be described by some number pair (*x*, *y*), where *x* locates its position along the *x*-coordinate axis and *y* locates its position along the *y*-coordinate axis. These (*x*, *y*) pairs form a coordinate system in the plane. The *x* and *y* axes are two intersecting number lines. Generally, *x* is the horizontal axis and *y* is the vertical axis. See Figure A-2. Also by convention, the first number of the number pair gives the *x*-coordinate. The second number of the pair gives the *y*-coordinate. This is called an *ordered pair*. Once this order has been established— usually *x* first, *y* second—it may not be changed.

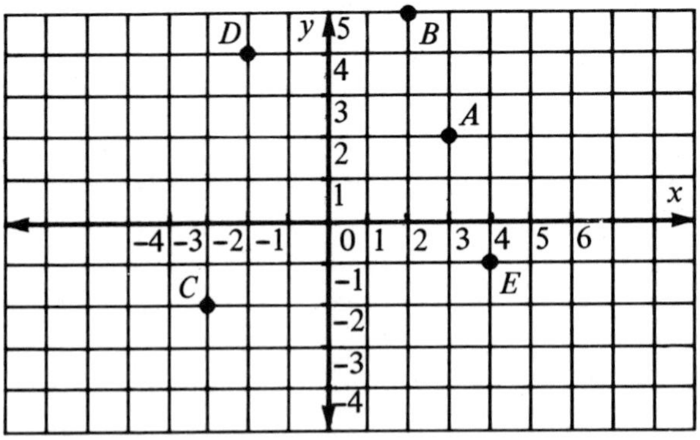

In Figure A-2, point *A* is located at *x*-3, *y*-2, or (3, 2).

B is at (__,__)

C is at (−3,__)

D is at (__,__)

E is at (__,__)

Figure A-2.

If you need practice plotting number pairs, plot the following set of number pairs; see what turns up. First, connect (1,1), (1,2), (4,2), (4,–1), (2,–4), (–1,–4), (–4,–2), (–4,6), (–1,9), (4,9), (4,7); then disconnect. Now start again; connect (–16,–4), (–15,9), (–11,1), (–7,9), (–6,–4); disconnect. Finally, connect (5,–4), (10,9), (15,–4), (13,1), (7,1). This figure will fit on centimeter or ¼ inch graph paper with the origin (intersection of x-axis and y-axis) at the center of the paper and each unit equal to 1.

Appendix 4
The Witch of Agnesi

A less crude method of generating the Witch of Agnesi is to calculate points F from the ratio equation, $\dfrac{TO}{TR} = \dfrac{TB}{RC}$.

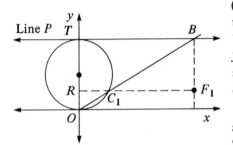

Figure A-3.

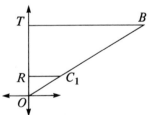

Figure A-4.

Figure A-3 shows the situation for C_1 at $(3,2)$. RF_1 is a line through C_1 and parallel to the x-axis. (It is also parallel to line P). Notice then that all points on RF_1 have the same y-coordinate. Therefore F_1 and C_1 have the same y-coordinate, since they are both points on line RF_1.

Figure A-4 is extracted from Figure A-3 and shows similar triangles TBO and RCO. Since TBO and RCO are similar triangles, it is true that $\dfrac{TO}{RO} = \dfrac{TB}{RC_1}$. We call this the *Ratio Equation.* From Figures 4-5 and A-3 we know that

$TO = 6$ (This is the diameter of the circle.)

$RO = 2$ (This is the y-coordinate of C_1. It is also the y-coordinate of F_1.)

$RC_1 = 3$ (This is the x-coordinate of C_1.)

Substituting these three values in the ratio, we can solve for TB. We want to do this since TB is the x-coordinate of F_1, and in order to locate F_1 we need to know both its x- and its y-coordinates.

$$\frac{6}{2} = \frac{TB}{3}$$

$$TB = \frac{6}{2} \times 3 = 9 \ (x\text{-coordinate of } F_1.)$$

Therefore when $C = (3,2)$ approximately, we know that $F = (9,2)$ approximately.

Complete Table A-1 below, using values for C from Figure A-5. Choose values of x and y that look from the diagram, like they are correct to within ¼ unit. This will be accurate enough for our purposes. For example, our readings give $C_1 = C_2 = C_3$, although we know this cannot be true. Reading them as equal will give us points F which will make our curve look good enough. From the symmetry of the circle we see that for each point F at (x,y) there is a point F' at $(-x,y)$.

Table A-1

C	For any $C(x_c, y)$		$\dfrac{6}{y}$	$x = \dfrac{6}{y} x_c$	$F(x,y)$	$F'(-x,y)$
	x_c(read RC)	y(read RO)				
C_1	3	2	3	9	(9,2)	(−9,2)
C_2						
C_3						
C_4						
C_5						
C_6						
C_7						

Plot points F and F' on Figure A-5, and see the Witch of Agnesi emerge again.

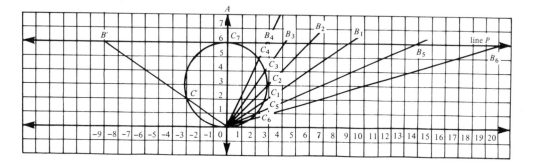

Figure A-5.

211

Extra for Experts

The following way to generate the Witch is not crude at all. We complete the derivation of the equation of the curve. Then F will be all (x,y) pairs which satisfy the equation. First we go back again to Figure A-4 and the ratio equation:

$$\frac{TO}{RO} = \frac{TB}{RC_1} \tag{1}$$

If the diameter of the circle is $2a$, $C=(x_c,y)$ and $F=(x,y)$, then

$TO = 2a$

$RO = y$ (That is, the y-coordinate of both C and F)

$TB = x$ (That is, the x-coordinate of F)

$RC = x_c$ (That is, the x-coordinate of C)

Substituting these values in the ratio equation, we have

$$\frac{2a}{y} = \frac{x}{x_c} \tag{2}$$

From the equation of a circle, $x_c^2 + (y-a)^2 = a^2$ we know that $x_c = \sqrt{a^2 - (y-a)^2}$. We use $(y-a)$ instead of Y here to account for the displacement of the circle in Figure 4-5, whose center is not at the origin. Substituting this value of x_c in equation (2) we get

$$\frac{2a}{y} = \frac{x}{\sqrt{a^2-(y-a)^2}} \ . \tag{3}$$

Squaring both sides of equation (3) and doing some other things, we get

$$\frac{4a^2}{y^2} = \frac{x^2}{a^2-(y-a)^2} = \frac{x^2}{a^2-y^2+2ay-a^2}$$

$$= \frac{x^2}{y(2a-y)}$$

and finally

$$x^2 y = 4a^2(2a-y)$$

which is the equation of the Witch of Agnesi. From this equation all values of x and y can be calculated. These (x,y) pairs are points F. All these points F form the curve known as the Witch of Agnesi.

Appendix 5
Two Elementary Constructions

A. Construct an equilateral triangle.

1. For any line AB, open compass to width AB.

2. With compass point at A, spin an arc. All points on this arc are distance AB from A.

3. With compass point at B, spin another arc. All points on this arc are also distance AB from B.

4. Call the intersection of these arcs C.

5. Connect AC and CB, forming $\triangle ACB$.

Triangle ACB is an equilateral triangle since $AC = CB = AB$. The three sides have been constructed to be equal.

B. Bisect an angle.

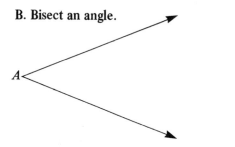

1. With compass point at A, draw any arc through rays of angle A.

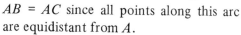

$AB = AC$ since all points along this arc are equidistant from A.

2. With compass point on B, spin any arc.

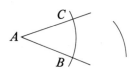

3. With compass point on *C*, spin an arc using the same compass opening as in step 2. All points on this arc are the same distance from *C* as all points of the arc with center at *B* are from *B*. Call this intersection *D*.

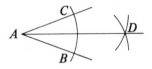

4. Draw line *AD*. Line *AD* is the bisector of angle *A*. Angle *DAB* = angle *DAC*. Do you see why?

Appendix 6
Isometric Grid

Appendix 7
Some Finite Difference Theory

The method of constant differences is generally introduced as a technique for teaching students to discover the function rule which will generate a desired sequence. A sequence that will generate a constant difference may be represented by a polynomial whose degree equals the number of times a difference sequence is obtained before the difference sequence becomes constant. For example, on page 113 the first sequence was 0, 1, 4, 9, 16, 25, 36, ... The first difference sequence was 1, 3, 5, 7, 9, 11, ... The second difference sequence was 2, 2, 2, 2, . . . a constant value. Therefore, the polynomial which describes this sequence is a second-degree polynomial of the form $ax^2 + bx + c$. If we determine the values of a, b, and c, we will have the desired function. But a is always half the value of the constant difference. In this example, $a = \frac{1}{2} \times 2 = 1$. And b is always the difference between the first value of the first difference sequence and A. In this case, where the first difference sequence begins 1, 3, 5, . . . , $b = 1 - a = 1 - 1 = 0$. Finally, c is always the first value of the first sequence; that is, the value of the function when $n = 0$. In this case, $c = 0$. Substituting $a = 1$, $b = 0$, and $c = 0$ into our general second-degree polynomial form, $ax^2 + bx + c$, we get $1 \cdot x^2 + 0 \cdot x + 0 = x^2 + 0 + 0 = x^2$, which equals $f(n)$ in this case. Using a similar technique, you can check the other functions by deriving $f(n)$ for each.

Appendix 8
The Pathological Snowflake

Can you understand the entries in the Table A-2, which evaluate the perimeter and area at each stage of the snowballing snowflake?

Table A-2

Construction	Number of sides	Length of side	Perimeter	Area
1	3	a	$3a$	$\dfrac{a^2\sqrt{3}}{4}$
2	$4 \cdot 3$	$\frac{1}{3}a$	$\frac{4}{3} \cdot 3a$	$\dfrac{a^2\sqrt{3}}{4} + \dfrac{a^2\sqrt{3}}{12}$
3	$4^2 \cdot 3$	$(\frac{1}{3})^2 a$	$(\frac{4}{3})^2 \cdot 3a$	$\dfrac{a^2\sqrt{3}}{4} + \dfrac{a^2\sqrt{3}}{12} + \dfrac{a^2\sqrt{3}}{27}$
4	$4^3 \cdot 3$	$(\frac{1}{3})^3 a$	$(\frac{4}{3})^3 \cdot 3a$	$\dfrac{a^2\sqrt{3}}{4} + \dfrac{a^2\sqrt{3}}{12} + \dfrac{a^2\sqrt{3}}{12}\left(\dfrac{4}{9}\right)$ $+ \dfrac{a^2\sqrt{3}}{12} \cdot \left(\dfrac{4}{9}\right)^2$
5	$4^4 \cdot 3$	$(\frac{1}{3})^4 a$	$(\frac{4}{3})^4 \cdot 3a$	$\dfrac{a^2\sqrt{3}}{4} + \displaystyle\sum_{x=1}^{4} \dfrac{a^2\sqrt{3}}{12}\left(\dfrac{4}{9}\right)^{x-1}$
n	$4^{n-1} \cdot 3$	$(\frac{1}{3})^{n-1} a$	$(\frac{4}{3})^{n-1} \cdot 3a$	$\dfrac{a^2\sqrt{3}}{4} + \displaystyle\sum_{x=1}^{n-1} \dfrac{a^2\sqrt{3}}{12}\left(\dfrac{4}{9}\right)^{x-1}$

Appendix 9
Some Formal Group Properties

A group is a structure which consists of a set of elements. These elements combine together in some defined way, two at a time. This combining by twos is called a *binary operation*. If such a set, with its binary operation, does indeed have the structure of a group, it will have four essential properties. These properties are:

1. Closure,
2. Associativity,
3. Identity element, and
4. Inverse elements.

Commutativity is an optional property. A group that has this fifth property is called a *commutative group*. Many groups do not have it.

These group properties are defined as follows:

1. *Closure:* This means that the combination of any two elements in the set under the set operation, * , will result in an element which is one of those in the original set. Such a set is said to be closed or to have closure. For example, whenever odd numbers are added (*), the result will be an odd number. Contrast this with the set of counting numbers under subtraction. This familiar set does not have closure; Table A-3 shows part of its combination table.

Table A-3

$-$	1	2	3	4	.	.	.
1	0	−1	−2	−3	.	.	.
2	1	0	−1	−2	.	.	.
3	2	1	0	−1	.	.	.
4	3	2	1	0	.	.	.
.	.	.	.	.	.	.	.
.	.	.	.	.	.	.	.

All the numbers enclosed in the curve are *outside* the initial set, which has been defined as numbers greater than or equal to one. These numbers are negative numbers and zero. Therefore, closure has been violated. We say that the counting numbers are not a group under subtraction since they are not closed under this operation.

The counting numbers do have closure under addition. Can you see why?

2. *Associativity:* This property says that the order in which more than two elements of a set are combined does not matter. In ordinary addition with whole numbers, we know that 2+3+4 may be added (2+3)+4=5+4=9 or 2+(3+4)=2+7=9. Therefore we say addition of whole numbers is associative.

Check different ways of combining the odd, even set until you are convinced it is also associative under addition. For example: $C+E+E$ can be combined $(O+E)+E$ or $O+(E+E)$. $(O+E)+E=O+E=O$ or $O+(E+E)=O+E=O$. Either way gives the same result.

3. *Identity element:* This refers to one element in the set which has a unique property. Any element combined with the identity element is unchanged.

In ordinary addition with whole numbers, zero is the identity element, since any number is unchanged when added to zero.

When multiplication is the operation and whole numbers the set, one is the identity element. Any number multiplied by one is unchanged.

In the set, $\{$odd, even$\}$ E(even) is the identity element since $E+O=O$, $O+E=O$, and $E+E=E$.

We know that O(odd) cannot be the identity element since $O+O=E$. This violates the definition.

4. *Inverse elements:* This property means that for each element in the set, there exists one element also in the set, which combines with it to equal the identity element. This element may be itself, or any other element in the set.

In the odd, even set each element is its own inverse. That is, $E+E=E$ (the identity element) and $O+O=E$ (the identity element).

From arithmetic, since 5 + ⁻5 = 0, 5 is the inverse of ⁻5 under addition, and vice versa. Also, since 5 × 1/5 = 1, 1/5 is the inverse of 5 under multiplication.

5. *Commutativity:* This property means that the order of elements under the set operation does not matter. For example, addition of whole numbers is commutative since 3+5=5+3 or 6+9≠9+6. By contrast, subtraction of whole numbers is not commutative, since 3–5≠5–3 and 6–9≠9–6. Under subtraction, the order *does* make a difference!

The odd-even example is commutative, since $E+O=O+E=O$.

Since group properties 1 through 5 hold for the odd-even example, we say that the set {odd, even} is a group under the operation of addition. It satisfies the group properties: it has closure, associativity, and an identity element (E), and each element has an inverse (E has E and O has O). In addition, it is a commutative group since $E+O=O+E$.

Appendix 10
The Women: A Summary

Hypatia—A.D. 370–415

Greek (Alexandrian)

Algebraist; head of Alexandrian neoplatonic school.

Wrote commentaries on Diophantus' *Arithmetica* and on Apollonius' *Conic Sections.*

Emilie du Châtelet—1706–1749

French

Major work: *Mathematical Principles of Natural Philosophy* (1759), a French translation and commentaries on Newton's *Principia.*

Also *Dissertation on the Nature and Propagation of Fire.*

Maria Agnesi—1718–1799

Italian

Major work: *Analytical Institutions* (1748), a complete, integrated treatment of algebra and analysis, with emphasis on concepts new to her time. The work includes many methods and generalizations original with her.

Sophie Germain—1776–1831

French

Number Theory and Analysis

Winner of important prize for formulation of mathematical theory of vibrations of general curved and plane elastic surfaces. Methodology involved calculus of variations.

Mary Somerville—1780–1872

English

Mathematical physicist; scientific expositor

Publications include:

The Mechanism of the Heavens (1831)

On the Connection of the Physical Sciences (1834)

Physical Geography (1848)

On Molecular and Microscopic Science (1869)

Also mathematical monographs such as *On Curves and Surfaces of Higher Orders.*

Ada Augusta Lovelace—1815–1852

English

"Inventor" of computer programming.

Worked with Charles Babbage on concepts relating to early computers.

Sonya Kovalevskaya—1850–1891

Russian

Complex analysis

Solved problem of rotation of a rigid body about a fixed point.

Generalized work of Euler, Poisson, and Lagrange, using hyperelliptic integrals to solve differential equations of motion.

Grace Chisholm Young—1868–1944

English

Set Theory

Special emphasis on applications of set theory to problems in mathematical analysis.

Emmy Noether—1882-1935

German

Investigation of structure of noncommutative algebras.

Formulated and developed the concept of primary ideals.

Suggested Readings and References

General

Campbell, Paul J. and Grinstein, Louise S., "Women in Mathematics: A Preliminary Selected Bibliography", *Philosophia Mathematica*, 1977.

Dictionary of Scientific Biography, Charles Coulston Gillespie (ed.), New York: Charles Scribner, 1972-1977. (Contains excellent articles and references on Agnesi, du Châtelet, Hypatia, Germain, Somerville, Kovalevskaya, and Noether).

Dubreil-Jacotin, Marie Louise, "Women Mathematicians" in *Great Currents of Mathematical Thought*, F. Le Lionnais (ed.). New York: Dover, 1971.

Ernest, John, "Mathematics and Sex", *American Mathematical Monthly*, October 1976, 83:595-615, or author, University of California at Santa Barbara.

Mozans, H. J., *Women in Science,* New York and London: D. Appleton and Co., 1913. Reissued, M. I. T. Press.

Osen, Lynn M., *Women in Mathematics*, Cambridge, Mass. and London, England: M. I. T. Press, 1974.

Hypatia
Kingsley, Charles, *Hypatia*, Chicago: E. A. Weeks & Co.

Du Châtelet

Edwards, Samuel, *The Divine Mistress,* New York: David McKay Co., 1970.
Mitford, Nancy, *Voltaire in Love*, New York: Harper & Bros., 1957.

Somerville

Somerville, Martha, *Personal Recollections of Mary Somerville*, Boston: Roberts Brothers, 1874.

Lovelace

Bernstein, Jeremy, *The Analytic Engine,* New York: Random House, 1963.
Moseley, Maboth, *Irascible Genius*, London: Hutchinson & Co. 1964.

Kovalevskaya

Kovalevskaya, Sonya, *Her Recollections of Childhood*, Transl. by Isabel F. Hapgood, New York: The Century Co., 1895.

Leffler, Anna Carlotta, *Sonya Kovalevsky*, London: T. Fisher Unwin, 1895.

Polubarinova-Kochina, P., *Sophia Vasilyevna Kovalevskaya, Her Life and Work*, Moscow: Foreign Languages Publishing House, 1957.

Young

Grattan-Guinness, Ivor, "A Mathematical Union: William Henry and Grace Chisholm Young", *Annals of Science,* 29:2, August 1972.

Young, Grace Chisholm, *Beginners Book of Geometry*, New York: Chelsea Publishing Co. 1970 (reprint).

Footnotes

Hypatia

[1] Charles Kingsley, *Hypatia* (Chicago: E. A. Weeks & Co.), p. 431.

[2] *Ibid.*, p. 445.

Du Châtelet

[1] Samuel Edwards, *The Divine Mistress* (New York: David McKay Co., 1970), Frontispage. Reprinted by permission.

[2] *Ibid.*, p. 4.

[3] *Ibid.*

[4] *Ibid.*, p. 15.

[5] *Ibid.*

[6] *Ibid.*, p. 81.

[7] Frank Hanel, *An Eighteenth Century Marquise* (New York: James Pott & Co., 1911), p. 368.

[8] Lynn Osen, *Women in Mathematics* (Cambridge, Mass: The M.I.T. Press, 1974), p. 68.

Agnesi

[1] Sarah Josepha Hale, *Women's Record* (New York: Harper & Bros., 1853), p. 160.

[2] Edna Kramer, "Agnesi, Maria Gaetana", *Dictionary of Scientific Biography,* ed. Charles Coulston Gillespie (New York: Scribners, 1972-1977), I, 76.

[3] Sister Mary Thomas à Kempis, "The Walking Polyglot", *Scripta Mathematica,* VI (1939), 215.

[4] Maria Agnesi, *Analytical Institutions,* English translation by Rev. J. Colson (London, 1801), Introduction.

[5] Kramer, *op. cit.,* p. 77.

[6] Colson, *loc. cit.*

[7] *Ibid.*

Germain

[1] Eric Temple Bell, "The Prince of Mathematicians", *The World of Mathematics,* ed. James R. Newman (New York: Simon & Shuster, 1956), I, 333.

[2] *Ibid*, p. 334.

Somerville

[1] Duncan Taylor, *Fielding's England* (New York: Roy Publishers, 1966), p. 92.

[2] Martha Somerville, *Personal Recollections of Mary Somerville* (Boston: Roberts Bros., 1874), pp. 18–19.

[3] *Ibid.,* p. 22.

[4] *Ibid.*

[5] *Ibid.,* pp. 27–28.

[6] *Ibid.,* p. 37.

[7] *Ibid.,* pp. 46–47.

[8] *Ibid.,* p. 53.

[9] *Ibid.,* p. 54.

[10] *Ibid.,* p. 80.

[11] *Ibid.,* p. 84.

[12] *Ibid.,* p. 88.

[13] *Ibid.,* pp. 163–164.

[14] *Ibid.,* p. 171.

[15] *Ibid.,* p. 206.

[16] *Ibid.,* pp. 217–218.

[17] *Ibid.,* p. 267.

[18] *Ibid.*

[19] *Ibid.,* p. 124.

[20] *Ibid.,* p. 344.

[21] *Ibid.,* p. 345.

[22] *Ibid.,* p. 347.

[23] *Ibid.,* p. 361.

[24] *Ibid.,* pp. 348–349.

[25] *Ibid.,* p. 364.

[26] Mary Somerville, *The Connection of the Physical Sciences* (New York: Harper & Bros., 1854), p. 3.

[27] Mary Somerville, *Mechanism of the Heavens* (London: John Murray, 1831), p. 47.

[28] *Ibid.,* p. 47.

[29] *Ibid.,* p. 48.

[30] Howard Eves, *In Mathematical Circles* (Boston: Prindle, Weber & Schmidt, 1969), 2, p. 24.

[31] Mary Somerville, *The Connection of the Physical Sciences* (New York: Harper & Bros., 1854), p. 140.

Lovelace

[1] Maboth Moseley, *Irascible Genius* (London: Hutchinson & Co., 1964), p. 157.

[2] Ethel Coburn Mayne, *Anne Isabella Lady Noel Byron* (New York: Charles Scribner, 1929). pp. 296–297.

[3] Martha Somerville, *Personal Recollections of Mary Somerville* (Boston: Roberts Bros., 1874), p. 154.

[4] Ada Lovelace letter to Charles Babbage, July 23, 1843, MSS. (British Museum) 37192, f. 337.

[5] A.L. to C.B., July 27, 1843. MSS. 37192, f. 393.

[6] Mayne, *op. cit.,* p. 477.

[7] A.L. to C.B., undated (between March 1838 and March 1839), MSS. 37191, f. 87.

[8] A.L. to C.B., January 12, 1841, MSS. 37191, f. 543.

[9] *Ibid.*

[10] A.L. to C.B., July 1843, MSS. 37192, f. 339.

[11] A.L. to C.B., July 28, 1843, MSS. 37192, f. 399.

[12] A.L. to C.B., August 14, 1843, MSS. 37192, f. 422.

[13] Moseley, *op. cit.,* p. 155.

[14] B.V. Bowden, *Faster Than Thought,* (London: Pitman & Sons, 1953), p. 367.

[15] *Ibid.,* p. 368.

[16] *Ibid.,* p. 365.

[17] *Ibid.,* p. 398.

[18] A.L. to C.B., February 16, 1840, MSS. 37191, f. 331.

Kovalevskaya

[1] Sonya Kovalévsky, *Her Recollections of Childhood,* Translated by Isabel F. Hapgood (New York: The Century Co., 1895), pp. 65–66.

[2] *Ibid.,* p. 66.

[3] *Ibid.,* p. 67.

[4] P. Polubarinova-Kochina, *Sophia Vasilyevna Kovalevskaya, Her Life and Work* (Moscow: Foreign Languages Publishing House, 1957), p. 27.

[5] Anna Carlotta Leffler, *Sonya Kovalevsky* (London: T. Fisher Unwin, 1895), pp. 22–23.

[6] *Ibid.*, p. 51.

[7] Polubarinova-Kochina, *op. cit.*, p. 50.

[8] Leffler, *op cit.* p. 69.

[9] *Ibid.*

[10] Leffler, *op cit.*, p. 64.

[11] Marie-Louise Dubreil-Jacotin, "Women Mathematicians", *Great Currents of Mathematical Thought,* ed. F. Le Lionnais (New York: Dover, 1971), I, 276.

[12] Polubarinova-Kochina, *op cit.*, p. 70.

[13] Kovelévsky, *op cit.*, p. 316.

Young

[1] I. Grattan-Guinness, "A Mathematical Union: William Henry and Grace Chisholm Young", *Annals of Science,* 29:2 (August, 1972), 107. Reprinted by permission of Taylor & Francis Ltd., London.

[2] *Ibid.*, p. 108.

[3] *Ibid.*

[4] *Ibid.*, p. 110.

[5] *Ibid.*, p. 121.

[6] *Ibid.*, p. 115.

[7] *Ibid.*, pp. 117–118.

[8] *Ibid.*, p. 123.

[9] *Ibid.*, p. 124.

[10] *Ibid.*, p. 125.

[11] *Ibid.*, pp. 127, 128.

[12] *Ibid.*, p. 129.

[13] *Ibid.*, p. 133.

[14] *Ibid.*, p. 135.

[15] *Ibid.*, p. 135.

[16] *Ibid.*, p. 141.

[17] *Ibid.*, p. 151.

[18] Grace Chisholm Young, *Beginner's Book of Geometry* (London, 1905. Reprinted: New York: Chelsea Publ. Co., 1970), Introduction.

[19] *Ibid.*, pp. 100, 101.

[20] *Ibid.*, p. 145.

[21] W.H. and G.C. Young, *The Theory of Sets and Points* (Cambridge, 1906. Reprinted: New York: Chelsea Publ. Co., Inc., 1972: 2nd Ed.), Introduction.

Noether

[1] Clark H. Kimberling, "Emmy Noether", *American Mathematical Monthly,* 79 (February, 1972), 137.

[2] Hermann Weyl, "Emmy Noether", *Scripta Mathematica*, VIII, 3 (July, 1935), 207.

[3] *Ibid.,* p. 208.

[4] *Ibid.,* p. 209.

[5] *Ibid.,* p. 210.

[6] Norbert Wiener, *I Am a Mathematician*, (New York: Doubleday & Co., 1956), p. 120.

[7] Kimberling, *op. cit.,* p. 148.

[8] Constance Reid, *Hilbert* (New York: Springer-Verlag, 1970), p. 143.

[9] Weyl, *op cit.,* p. 220.

[10] Kimberling, *op cit.,* p. 136. This quote is attributed by Constance Reid, *Hilbert,* p. 166, to the Russian mathematician Alexandroff.

The Problem

[1] Elizabeth Patterson, "Mary Somerville", *British Journal for History of Science,* 4:16 (1969), p. 318.

[2] Ada Lovelace letter to Charles Babbage, July 27, 1843, MSS. 37192, f. 393.

[3] John Tipper, ed. *Ladies Diary,* 1727, Preface.

[4] Taped interview with author, Berkeley, Ca., September 5, 1976.

[5] Charles H. Kimberling, "Emmy Noether", *American Mathematical* Monthly, 79 (February, 1972), 137.

Solutions

Meet The Women
Page 2 Hidden Mathematicians Puzzle

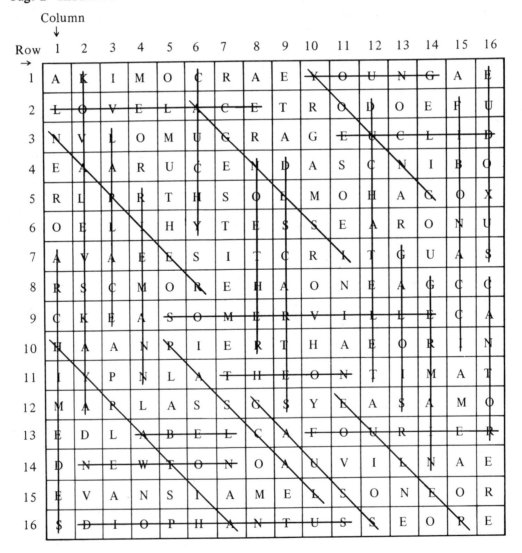

	Col 1	2	3	4	5	6	7	8	9	10	11	12	13	14	15	16
Row 1	A	K	I	M	O	C	R	A	E	Y	O	U	N	G	A	E
2	L	O	V	E	L	A	C	E	T	R	O	D	O	E	F	U
3	N	V	L	O	M	U	G	R	A	G	E	U	C	L	I	D
4	E	A	A	R	U	C	E	D	A	S	C	N	I	B	O	
5	R	L	R	T	H	S	O	E	M	O	H	A	C	O	X	
6	O	E	L	H	Y	T	E	S	S	E	A	R	O	N	U	
7	A	V	E	S	I	T	C	R	I	T	G	U	A	S		
8	R	S	C	M	O	R	E	H	A	O	N	E	A	G	C	C
9	C	K	E	A	S	O	M	E	R	V	I	L	L	E	C	A
10	H	A	A	N	R	I	E	R	T	H	A	E	O	R	I	N
11	I	K	P	N	L	A	T	H	E	O	N	T	I	M	A	T
12	M	A	R	L	A	S	S	G	S	Y	E	A	S	A	M	O
13	E	D	L	A	B	E	L	C	A	F	O	U	R	E	R	
14	D	N	E	W	T	O	N	O	A	U	V	I	L	N	A	E
15	E	V	A	N	S	I	A	M	E	L	S	O	N	E	O	R
16	S	D	I	O	P	H	A	N	T	U	S	S	E	O	R	E

230

Table 1-1.

	A (*W,M*)	B (Row, Column)	C (Row, Column)		A (*W,M*)	B (Row, Column)	C (Row, Column)
Abel	M	13,4	13,7	Germain	W	8,14	15,14
Agnesi	W	2,6	7,11	Hypatia	W	10,1	16,7
Archimedes	M	7,1	16,1	Kovalevskaya	W	1,2	12,2
Cantor	M	8,16	13,16	Laplace	M	3,3	(9,3)
Cauchy	M	1,6	6,6	Lovelace	W	2,2	2,8
Descartes	M	4,9	12,9	Napier	M	3,1	8,6
Diophantus	M	(16,2)	16,11	Newton	M	14,2	14,7
Du Châtelet	W	2,12	11,12	Noether	W	4,8	10,8
Euclid	M	3,11	3,16	Pascal	M	10,5	15,10
Eudoxus	M	1,16	7,16	Riemann	M	5,4	11,4
Euler	M	12,11	16,15	Somerville	W	9,5	9,14
Fibonacci	M	2,15	10,15	Theon	M	11,7	11,12
Fourier	M	(13,10)	(13,16)	Young, G. C.	W	1,10	1,14
Galois	M	7,13	12,13	Young, W. H.	M	1,10	5,14
Gauss	M	12,8	16,12				

Page 4 Composite: 3 × 5; 1 × 15.

Table 1-2.

	Number of letters in first name	Prime or Composite?	Number of letters in last name	Prime or Composite?	Number of letters in complete name	Prime or Composite?
Hypatia	7	P	–	–	7	P
Emilie du Châtelet	6	C	10	C	16	C
Maria Agnesi	5	P	6	C	11	P
Sophie Germain	6	C	7	P	13	P
Mary Somerville	4	C	10	C	14	C
Ada Lovelace	3	P	8	C	11	P
Sonya Kovalevskaya	5	P	12	C	17	P
Grace Young	5	P	5	P	10	C
Emmy Noether	4	C	7	P	11	P

Page 5

$P_1 = \begin{cases} \text{Hypatia} & \underline{\hspace{6cm}} \\ \text{Maria (Agnesi)} & \underline{\hspace{6cm}} \\ \text{Ada (Lovelace)} & \underline{\hspace{6cm}} \\ \text{Sonya (Kovalevskaya)} & \underline{\hspace{6cm}} \\ \text{Grace (Young)} & \underline{\hspace{6cm}} \end{cases}$

$P_2 = \begin{cases} \text{(Sophie) Germain} & \underline{\hspace{6cm}} \\ \text{(Grace) Young} & \underline{\hspace{6cm}} \\ \text{(Emmy) Noether} & \underline{\hspace{6cm}} \\ & \underline{\hspace{6cm}} \\ & \underline{\hspace{6cm}} \end{cases}$

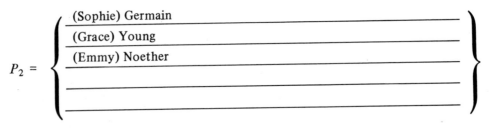

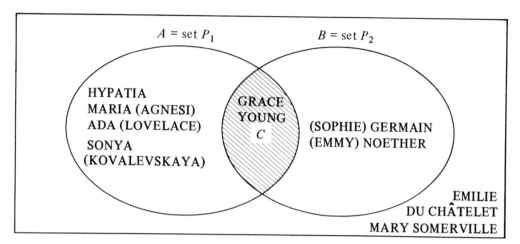

Figure 1-1.

Page 6

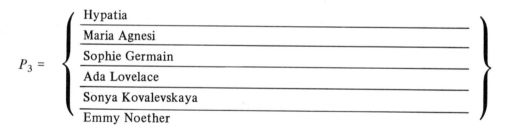

$P_3 = \left\{ \begin{array}{l} \text{Hypatia} \\ \text{Maria Agnesi} \\ \text{Sophie Germain} \\ \text{Ada Lovelace} \\ \text{Sonya Kovalevskaya} \\ \text{Emmy Noether} \end{array} \right\}$

233

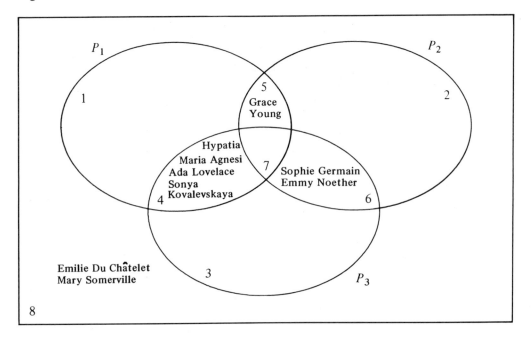

Figure 1-2.

Hypatia

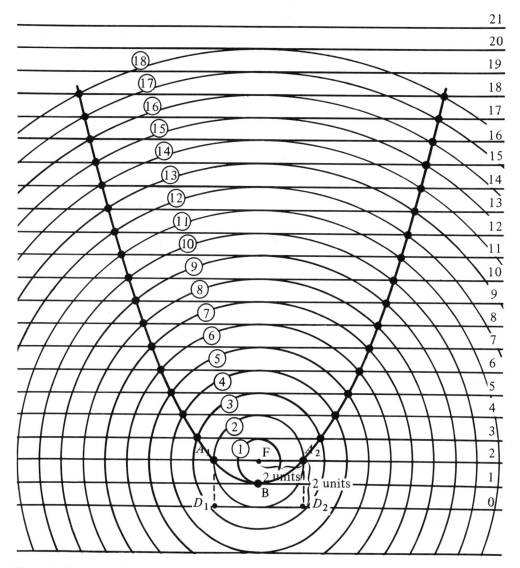

Figure 2-6.

Page 22 (continued)

ellipse
2 units from F_1; 2 units long
7 units from F_2; 7 units long

Page 24 *intersection* of ③ and ⑥
concentric circles
centers at F_1; F_2
3 units; *6* units

Emilie du Châtelet

Page 41 In 1 seconds, 16 feet
In 2 seconds, 64 feet
In 3 seconds, 144 feet
Page 43 time; distance
post office to Anne's house: 10 miles
swimming pool from Jay's house: 6 miles
library to post office: 2 hours
firehouse to swimming pool: 1 hour 20 minutes
Page 44 *4* miles; *80* minutes; $\dfrac{4 \text{ miles}}{80 \text{ minutes}} = 3 \dfrac{\text{miles}}{\text{hour}}$

Table 3-2.

Distance between points / Time of walk between points	Anne's house	Fire-house	Library	Swim-ming pool	City hall	Post office	Jay's house
Anne's house	X	2/40	4/80	6/120	8/160	10/200	12/240
Firehouse	2/40	X	2/40	4/80	6/120	8/160	10/200
Library	4/80	2/40	X	2/40	4/80	6/120	8/160
Swimming pool	6/120	4/80	2/40	X	2/40	4/80	6/120
City hall	8/160	6/120	4/80	2/40	X	2/40	4/80
Post office	10/200	8/160	6/120	4/80	2/40	X	2/40
Jay's house	12/240	10/200	8/160	6/120	4/80	2/40	X

$$\text{velocity} = \frac{1}{10} \frac{\text{miles}}{\text{minute}} ; \frac{6 \text{ miles}}{\text{hour}}$$

Page 46

Table 3-3.

Points of interest	Distance (miles) from Anne's house.	Δd (change in distance)	Time (minutes) from Anne's house	Δt (change in time)	Velocity $\Delta d/\Delta t$ (miles/minute)
A Anne's house	0		0		
B Firehouse	2	2 —	40	40 —	2/40
C Library	4	2	80	40	2/40
D Swimming pool	6	2	90	10	2/10
E Swimming pool	6	0	140	50	0
F City hall	8	2	150	10	2/10
G Post office	10	2	160	10	2/10
H Jay's house	12	2	200	40	2/40

0 miles/minute; swimming
2/40 miles/minutes; walking
2/10 miles/minute; biking

Page 47 20 feet; 16 feet; 5 feet
Page 48 At C, 19 feet; at D, 15 feet.
Δd = 4 ft; Δt = .3 seconds

Page 50

T H E I N C R E A S I N G   R A D I I   A P P R O A C H A   L I M I T.
1 2 3   4 5 6 7 3 8 9 4 5 15   7 8 10 4 4   8 11 11 7 14 8 6 2   8   13 4 12 4 1

Figure 3-8.

237

Maria Gaetana Agnesi

Page 61

Table 4-1.

C	Coordinates of points F		Coordinates of points F'	
	x (Read x-coordinate of B)	y (Read y-coordinate of c)	x' (read $-x$)	y' (same as y)
C_1	9	2	-9	2
C_2	6	3	-6	3
C_3	4	4	-4	4
C_4	3	5	-3	5
C_5	14	1	-14	1
C_6	20	.5	-20	.5
C_7	0	6	0	6

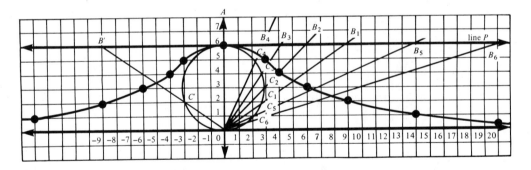

Figure 4-5.

238

Sophie Germain

Page 69

Table 5-1.

Column	1	2	3	4
Row	x	$k_1 \bmod(3)$	$k_2 \bmod(5)$	$k_3 \bmod(7)$
1	5	2	0	5
2	7	1	2	0
3	8	2	3	1
4	9	<u>0</u>	4	<u>2</u>
5	10	1	<u>0</u>	<u>3</u>
6	12	<u>0</u>	2	5
7	15	<u>0</u>	<u>0</u>	<u>1</u>

$x \equiv k \bmod(p)$

Table 5-2.

1	2	3	4	5	6	7	8	9	10	11	12	13	14
			$x^3 \bmod(p)$; p is a prime						$x^4 \bmod(p)$; p is a prime				
x	x^2	x^3	3	5	7	11	13	x^4	3	5	7	11	13
0	0	0	0	0	0	0	0	0	0	0	0	0	0
1	1	1	1	1	1	1	1	1	1	1	1	1	1
2	4	8	2	3	1	8	8	16	1	1	2	5	3
3	9	27	0	2	6	5	1	81	0	1	4	4	3
4	16	64	1	4	1	9	12	256	1	1	4	3	9
5	25	125	2	0	6	4	8	625	1	0	2	9	1
6	36	216	0	1	6	7	8	1296	0	1	1	9	9
7	49	343	1	3	0	2	5	2401	1	1	0	3	9
8	64	512	2	2	1	6	5	4096	1	1	1	4	1
9	81	729	0	4	1	3	1	6561	0	1	2	5	9
10	100	1000	1	0	6	10	12	10000	1	0	4	1	3
11	121	1331	2	1	1	0	5	14641	1	1	4	0	3
12	144	1728	0	3	6	1	12	20736	0	1	2	1	1
13	169	2197	1	2	6	8	0	28561	1	1	1	5	0

Page 72

Table 5-3

P	A solution exists for	
	$X^3 \equiv 2 \bmod(p)$	$X^4 \equiv 2 \bmod(p)$
3	yes: $2^3 = 8 \equiv 2 \bmod(3)$	no
5	yes: $3^3 = 27 \equiv 2 \bmod(5)$	no
7	no	yes: $2^4 = 16 \equiv 2 \bmod(7)$ also $5^4 = 625 \equiv 2 \bmod(7)$
11	yes $7^3 = 343 = 2 \bmod(11)$	no
12	no	no

Page 79

Table 5-4.

Figure	Name	Number of faces	Number of edges	Number of vertices
	tetrahedron	4	6	4
	cube	6	12	8
	octahedron	8	12	6

Mary Somerville

Page 98

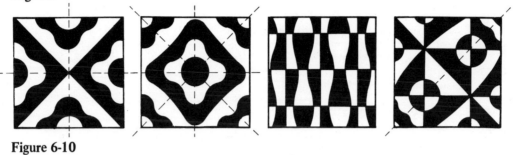

Figure 6-10

Lines of Reflection
Symmetry

Uncolored	4	4	2	2
Colored	2	4	0	1

Ada Byron Lovelace

Page 113 Table 7-3 will be the same as Table 7-2.

Page 115

Table 7-4.

Row

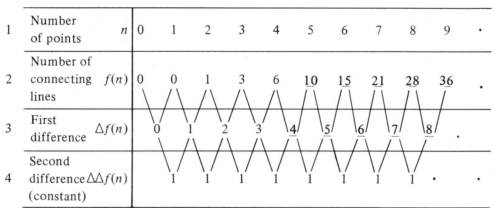

Table 7-5.

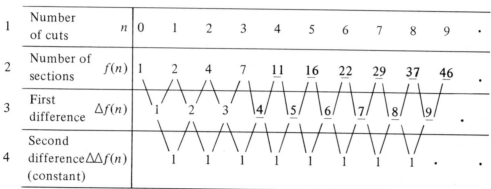

Row														
1	Number of cuts	n	0	1	2	3	4	5	6	7	8	9	.
2	Number of sections	$f(n)$	1	2	4	7	11	16	22	29	37	46	.
3	First difference	$\Delta f(n)$		1	2	3	4	5	6	7	8	9	.
4	Second difference $\Delta\Delta f(n)$ (constant)				1	1	1	1	1	1	1	1	. .

Table 7-6.

Row														
1		n	0	1	2	3	4	5	6	7	8	9	.
2		$f(n)$	0	1	4	10	20	35	56	84	120	165	.
3		$\Delta f(n)$		1	3	6	10	15	21	28	36	45	.
4		$\Delta\Delta f(n)$			2	3	4	5	6	7	8	9	. .
5	Constant difference	$\Delta\Delta\Delta f(n)$				1	1	1	1	1	1	1	. . .

Page 121

Table 7-7.

Row

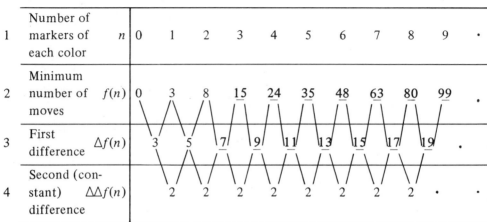

		n	0	1	2	3	4	5	6	7	8	9	•
1	Number of markers of each color												
2	Minimum number of moves	$f(n)$	0	3	8	15	24	35	48	63	80	99	•
3	First difference	$\Delta f(n)$		3	5	7	9	11	13	15	17	19	•
4	Second (constant) difference	$\Delta\Delta f(n)$			2	2	2	2	2	2	2	2	•

Page 124

Table 7-8.

Row

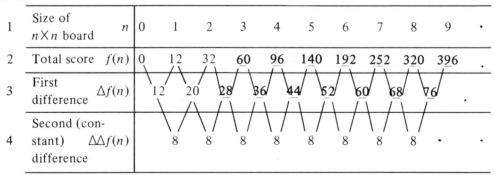

		n	0	1	2	3	4	5	6	7	8	9	•
1	Size of $n \times n$ board												
2	Total score	$f(n)$	0	12	32	60	96	140	192	252	320	396	•
3	First difference	$\Delta f(n)$		12	20	28	36	44	52	60	68	76	•
4	Second (constant) difference	$\Delta\Delta f(n)$			8	8	8	8	8	8	8	8	•

Sonya Kovalevskaya

Page 140 Minimum number of moves: 0, 1, 3, 7, 15, 31, 63, . . .
Page 142 $2^{64} - 1 = 18{,}446{,}744{,}073{,}709{,}551{,}615$ seconds.

Table 8-2.

Adjacent terms $f(n), f(n\text{-}1)$	Sequence of ratios between adjacent terms $f(n) \div f(n\text{-}1)$
2,1	2÷1 =2
3,2	3÷2 =1.5
5,3	5÷3 =1.66
8,5	8÷5 =1.60
13,8	13÷8 =1.625
21,13	21÷13 =1.615
34,21	34÷21 =1.619
55,34	55÷34 =1.6177
89,55	89÷55 =1.6182
144,89	144÷89 =1.61798
233,144	233÷144=1.61806
377,233	377÷233=1.61803

Grace Chisholm Young

Page 167

Table 9-1.

Figure	Number of edges (E)	Number of vertices (V)	Number of faces (F)
9-1	12	8	6
9-2	9	6	5
9-3	6	4	4
9-4	9	6	5
9-5	12	6	8
9-6	18	8	12

$V + F = E + 2$

Emmy Noether

Page 180

Table 10-3.

$\times$	E	O
E	E	E
O	E	O

Page 181

Table 10-4.

$\oplus$	0	1	2
0	0	1	2
1	1	2	0
2	2	0	1

Table 10-5.

$\oplus$	0	1	2	3	4	5
0	0	1	2	3	4	5
1	1	2	3	4	5	0
2	2	3	4	5	0	1
3	3	4	5	0	1	2
4	4	5	0	1	2	3
5	5	0	1	2	3	4

Tables 10-6, 10-7, 10-8 are all the same.

*	I	J	K	L	M	N
I	I	J	K	L	M	N
J	J	K	I	M	N	L
K	K	I	J	N	L	M
L	L	N	M	I	K	J
M	M	L	N	J	I	K
N	N	M	L	K	J	I

Hidden Mathematicians Puzzle—Contemporary Women

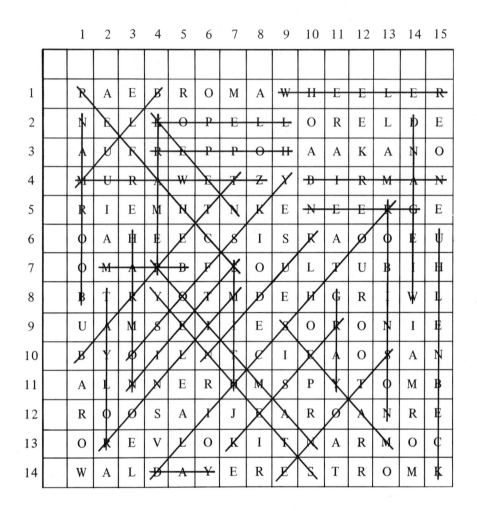

Table 11-1

Contemporary Women Mathematicians	A	B	Their Fields
Barrett, Lida	10,1	4,7	Topology; applied mathematics
Birman, Joan	4,10	4,15	Algebra; topology
Blum, Lenore	1,4	4,1	Logic and foundations; algebra and theory of numbers; applied mathematics
Boorman, Evelyn	8,1	2,1	Algebra; theory of numbers
Bram, Leila	7,5	7,2	Analytic number theory
Day, Jane	14,4	14,6	Algebra and theory of numbers; topology; Topological semigroups
Elkins, Judith	1,14	6,9	Analysis; complex variables; approximation theory
Gray, Mary	8,11	11,11	Algebra and theory of numbers
Green, Judy	5,14	5,10	Logic and foundations
Harmon, Adelaide	6,3	11,3	Mathematics education
Hopper, Grace	3,9	3,4	Computer science
Keen, Linda	2,4	5,7	Analysis
Kopell, Nancy	2,4	2,9	Applied math; analysis
Kramer, Edna	2,4	7,4	Algebra and theory of numbers; analysis; applied math; statistics and probability
Mayes, Vivienne	13,13	9,9	Algebra and theory of numbers
Milnor, Tilla	8,7	13,2	Geometry
Morawetz, Cathleen	4,1	4,8	Applied math
Osofsky, Barbara	10,3	4,9	Algebra and theory of numbers; Logic and foundations
Resek, Diane	9,11	14,4	Logic and foundations
Robinson, Julia	5,13	12,13	Number theoretical decision problems; recursive functions
Roitman, Judith	7,4	13,10	Logic and foundations; set theory; topology
Rothschild, Linda	5,13	14,4	Analysis; geometry
Rudin, Mary Ellen	6,10	10,6	Topology
Schafer, Alice	7,7	1,1	Algebra and theory of numbers; geometry
Smith, Martha	7,7	11,7	Algebra and theory of numbers
Stehney, Ann	14,10	8,4	Geometry
Stein, Marjorie	7,7	11,3	Linear systems; discrete math
Stone, Dorothy M.	10,13	14,9	Analysis
Taylor, Jean	8,2	12,2	Analysis; geometry
Uhlenbeck, Karen	1,15	14,15	Infinite dimensional differential topology; analysis
Wheeler, Mary	1,9	1,15	Applied math; analysis; numerical analysis
Wiegand, Sylvia	8,14	2,14	Abstract algebra

Illustration Credits